BOOKS BY EXOTIC ADRIAN STREET

SHAKE WRESTLE 'N' ROLL - SEMI FICTION - Copyright 1987

AUTOBIOGRAPHY

MY PINK GAS MASK - Copyright 2012

I ONLY LAUGH WHEN IT HURTS - Copyright 2012

SO MANY WAYS TO HURT YOU - Copyright 2012

SADIST IN SEQUINS - Copyright 2012

IMAGINE WHAT I COULD DO TO YOU - Copyright 2013

VIOLENCE IS GOLDEN - Copyright 2015

MERCHANT OF MENACE

By Adrian Street

Contact Information:

U.S. Mailing Address:

Adrian Street
1496 Oak Drive
Gulf Breeze, FL 32563

Email: daffodil777@bellsouth.net

Website: http://www.bizarebazzar.com

ISBN-13: 978-1518881473
ISBN-10: 1518881475

Cover:
Miss Linda & 'Exotic' Adrian - The Deadliest Duo in Wrestling.

In loving memory of my mother

DEDICATIONS:

My lovely Wife & Soul-mate Linda, in this World & the next -
the very best part of my journey of a lifetime.

To everyone who told me I couldn't do it - I couldn't have done it
without you.

Jeremy Deller - Artist.

Eddie Rose - Author of 'Send in the Clowns.'

Dale Storm - Author of 'Ask him again ref.'

Rupert Smith - Author of 'Man's World.'

Victor Rook - Author of 'People
Who Need To Die.'

Don Woods - my music man.

Jean - Adrian - Vince - Amanda - Gary - Chloe - Taylor -
Tallulah-Mae - Pam - Mike - Tina - Ollie.

Wrestling Heritage & Wrestling Furnace - Whose great websites
have immortalized
THE GOLDEN AGE OF PROFESSIONAL WRESTLING.

Russell Plummer - Ray Plunkett - Ken Sowden.

To every wrestler I ever stepped into the ring with, whether you
were the very worst, or the very best. I learned from you all.

The reason I love success and fame is, that it rewards both friends
and enemies in the manner they both deserve.

INTRODUCTION

My book has been self written and self edited - there may be mistakes - the only time I spent in Oxford or Cambridge was when I wrestled there. Throughout my life I have only done things one way - my way.

So for better or worse, This is my story.

MERCHANT OF MENACE

I'm The Merchant of Menace, purveyor of pain,
no quality of mercy is the name of my game.
I'll get my pound of flesh with every strangle hold.
To me all that glitters is definitely gold.

My curtains are the ropes, my stages are the rings,
the canvas is the scenery, the corners are the wings.
My scripts are all identical, the lines are very few.
I always play the leading man - and leading Lady too.

You'll get it as you like it, every time I hear the bell.
I can be like Romeo and Juliet as well.
As for Anthony and Cleo, I come somewhere in between.
I'm what I would call a Midsummer Night's Dream.

I'm the Merchant of Menace, purveyor of pain,
no quality of mercy is the name of my game.
I'll get my pound of flesh with every strangle hold.
To me all that glitters is definitely Gold.

I'm a Wrestler and an Actor, pursuing two careers.
I'm a brilliant thespian with cauliflower ears.
My theatres are the noisy halls, with benches made of wood,
My audience eat popcorn, while screaming out for blood.

When there are no more bones to break and no more ribs to
crack,
I'll bow to my admirers at the end of every act.
I'm a Gladiator who doesn't need a sword,
I nominate myself for an academy award.

I'm The Merchant of Menace, purveyor of pain,
no quality of mercy is the name of my game.
I'll get my pound of flesh with every strangle hold.
To me all that glitters is definitely Gold.

TENNESSEE 1985

Well we were back in Tennessee, and both as sick as a pair of bright Green Parrots. We had just been fired by Mid-South Booker, 'Superstar' Bill Dundee, as a result of giving him a rough time of it. That was my final contest in that territory.

It was Christmas 1984, one of the worst either of us had ever experienced. We both had chronically sore throats, which we attempted to soothe with bottle after bottle of Brandy. We had tried to rent an apartment in a complex where we had lived during previous tours of Tennessee, but everything was closed until after Christmas. Damn that was a miserable time.

We had our first contest on Memphis TV on the 29th of December, then our second contest at the Coliseum on New Year's Eve. By the beginning of 1985 we began to recover our health.

We found to our delight that Tennessee had a new booker. An old friend from Los Angeles, Tom Renesto. It was great to see him again, even better we didn't have to deal with 'Superstar' Dundee or 'The King' Jerry Lawler. I began by wrestling against various 'Good Guys' until one night when 'Hot Stuff' Eddie Gilbert came into my dressing room with a 'warning.'

"They are going to begin a program with you and the 'Macho-Man'," he told me, "I just thought I ought to warn you." he added ominously.

"Why do you need to warn me?" I inquired.

"Well I've been wrestling with him every night, I hate wrestling him, thank goodness you're going to wrestle him instead of me. I've had him up to here!" he added, reaching way up towards the ceiling, while standing on tiptoe.

"What's wrong with him?" I asked.

"Everything!" he replied, "You can never tell what he's going to do next - he's a complete nut case. They figure you're the only one in the territory who can handle him. No one else can control him. Every time I wrestle him he throws Coca-Cola all over me, and literally beats the fuckin' shit outa me! Thank goodness I won't be wrestling with him anymore "

"Where is he?" I asked.

I found that Randy Savage always used his own private dressing room.

'All the better.' I thought.

I had never met him before that night, I walked into his dressing room and introduced myself. I then got straight to the point.

"I've been told we are going to start a program against each other." I stated.

"Yeah - I heard that too." he replied.

"I've also been warned that you are completely off the fucking wall - which is okay with me - except I must warn you, that I would take extreme exception to you throwing anything like Coca-Cola at me during our contests. I pay a lot of money for my ring wear, and I don't want any of it ruined by having anything splashed over it."

"Yeah sure - that's okay." he assured me.

"I've also been told that you can be very tough and aggressive," I added, "And that's great - just the way I like it."

Well we began our program, and we really had some WILD BATTLES. Randy had been described by Lance Russell as being 'PURE ATHLETE.' and I would certainly have to agree - but Randy was not a wrestler.

I am certain that that statement is going to cause a lot of argument, and not a little controversy. But before you outright disagree with me, at least check out all the TV contests he had against me. Randy was pure Athlete, and he could certainly look after himself in a fight, but he couldn't wrestle. You have never seen him apply anything but the simplest of wrestling holds. Or escape from one.

'Macho-Man' Randy Savage had a reputation for his contribution to VERY exciting contests. BUT - if I wrestled him by blinding him with science, it would waste that essential reputation. Instead I decided to take the advice I had been given by 'Superstar' Bill Dundee, that I had more or less disregarded at the time I had received it.

'The Tennessee Territory thrives on 'Chicken-Shit' heels.' he had advised. I chose not to go that route the first time I wrestled in Tennessee, but this time I appreciated its value.

If I had chosen to, I was very capable of breaking Randy's arms, legs, or neck. I was a wrestler - he was not. BUT - if I chose to take the advice given to me by Dundee when I had wrestled against him, I could see the possibilities.

If I went into the ring and merely wasted Randy, I would also waste a great reputation that every fan believed in. If on the other hand I made it appear that I was afraid to come to grips with The Macho-Man, the possibilities were endless. So, instead of purposely showing up Randy's lack of wrestling skill, I would pretend that I was afraid to come to grips. I would duck, dive, run, hide behind Linda, even to the extent of placing Linda in harm's way, rather than come to grips with 'Macho-Man' Randy Savage myself. If I had come to grips from the start, there was two ways we could have continued - one we could have traded punches and kicks, which was basically the 'Macho-Man's style. Or we could actually wrestle, which would demonstrate my superiority, but diminish Randy's credibility. Randy's credibility could only be maintained, even enhanced, if I ran.

It was all smoke and mirrors, because when ever Randy caught me, Linda would lower the boom. If he turned from me to Linda then it would be me who 'Pearl Harbored' him. If you have never seen the videos, check some of them out, you will really appreciate what I am now describing. Instead of outwrestling 'The Macho-Man' as I could have done very easily, I played His game, and eventually beat him at his own game too. With a little help from Linda of course.

Well we wrestled each other night after night. Our matches generated so much excitement that we even carried our feud to Cape Gerardo, in Missouri, that was promoted by Randy's Father, Angelo Poffo. The climax took place in Memphis.

After our patent introduction, and very much mauling of 'The Macho-Man' by both Linda and I, who vied with each other who was going to deliver the most grievous bodily harm. Then Randy made his big comeback, which climaxed with him leaping off one of the ring-posts onto my head while I was outside the ring. This smashed me down onto the concrete floor of the arena and temporarily, completely put me out of the picture. Then Randy decided to get his revenge on Linda for the dozen or so kickings she had given him throughout the contest. He chased her all around the ring, Linda tried to escape by diving into the ring, but 'The Macho-Man' just managed to grab her by the ankle, which he used to haul himself into the ring. Once he had hold of Linda, he put her in position to deliver a devastating pile-driver. The bloodthirsty fans roared their approval, they wanted to see Linda get her comeuppance. Randy raised his hand to acknowledge the fans request. BIG MISTAKE! His triumphant gesture just gave me those extra vital seconds more to recover. I was in the ring and rang his bell, just as he was in the act of smashing Linda's head into the hard unyielding ring. I then grabbed him by his hair, tore him off the ground and hurled him in a summersault into the ropes. The 'Macho-Man' ended up with his neck entangled between the two top ropes and completely at my mercy. And as you all know, when it comes to wrestling 'Violence is Golden' and I don't have any mercy.

I battered The Macho-Man's face over and over - again, again and again. Blood began to spurt - everything around us got splashed. The referee tried to intervene, he got tossed aside. Linda leapt about keeping the ref at bay, while I continued to beat a savage tempo on The Macho-Man's face, which was now a scarlet mask. I got a warning from Linda that advised me that both the Batten Twins were entering the ring, in an attempt to rescue Bloody Randy. A few powerful kicks and punches took care of the both of them. Then I went back to work, savaging Savage. The Twins tried again - again I battered them off the ring apron before they could enter the ring. More battering for Savage. Lanny Poffo, Randy's Brother rushed to ringside, but he wisely thought better of entering it. Then while I was still pounding away, Boss man Eddie Marlin came to the timekeeper's table. He grabbed the microphone and threatened me with instant suspension if I struck the helpless Macho-Man just one more time. Shame - I was just getting warmed up.

It took Lanny and the Batten Twins to carry the Bloody unconscious Macho-Man back to his dressing room, after first prizing his head from between the ropes.

"WHERE'S YOUR MACHO-MAN NOW?!!!" I asked all the screaming fans after grabbing the microphone off Lance Russell's table. I hurled it back at him, before I strode triumphantly back to the dressing room.

It was just a couple of weeks later that Randy came into our dressing room to tell us that he had received a call from Vince McMahon Jr. I will soon be wrestling for the WWF he told us.

"Vince wants me to do your gimmick." he told me.

"They are going to change you from a 'Macho-Man' to a 'Macho-Queen' - sounds like Vince." I replied.

"No, not the sissy stuff," he assured me, "but he wants me to wear fancy robes like you, and go into the ring with a Lady Valet - just like you."

As soon as Jerry Lawler heard that Randy was going to wrestle for the WWF, he stole him from me. I imagined that Randy and I would be wrestling against each other right up until the time he was due to work for Vince. But true to form 'Jerry the King' wanted his victories over anyone who was going to be a main event feature for the WWF.

They had a brief feud - Randy was managed by an old friend of mine, Jeff Walton from Los Angeles. First they brutalized The King, then he avenged himself before the 'Macho-Man' went on to bigger and better things.

Meeting up with Jeff Walton again reminded Linda and I how much we had enjoyed living in Los Angeles and our regular visits from there to Las Vegas.

It was only a few months since my oldest Son, Adrian had come over for a too brief visit, and we were missing him already. We hadn't seen my other two children Vincent and Amanda since we were last in London. That was in November 1982, it was now April 1985. I decided to bring them all over to spend a holiday with us, and thought that Los Angeles and Las Vegas would be the very best place to spend some quality time together.

LOS ANGELES - LAS VEGAS

CALIFORNIA - HERE WE COME - RIGHT BACK WHERE WE STARTED FROM.

Linda and I flew out to Los Angeles on the 12th of April a few days ahead of my kids, who would be arriving on the 15th. We wanted those few days in order to make sure that everything would be 'Ship shape and Bristol fashion' when they did arrive.

We would all be staying with an old friend, Jimmy Maslon [who's pictured on the front cover of my 6th book 'Violence is Golden.]

Jimmy lived in one terrific house in the Hollywood Hills, it was situated just below the famous 'HOLLYWOOD SIGN.' On a clear day you could look right over the city of Los Angeles, and even see Catalina Island way out in the Pacific. Jimmy picked us up at the airport. On our drive from there, he told me that there was a very large store [I think it was called 'The Factory'] who after hearing that I was returning to L.A. for a few weeks, inquired if I would be willing to promote a Giant Sale they were having there. As the fee they offered was extremely generous, I was more than happy to oblige. Good that I did, as it got better and better.

I was paid extra for doing a radio commercial, and then a TV commercial. It drew a lot of customers to the store, and also the attention of 'Rhino Records' who offered me a record and video deal for some of the songs I had recorded and music videos I had produced. Then it got better still.

By the time I was to appear at 'The Factory,' my Kids had arrived in L.A. and were already with Linda and I. The Factory required that after my introduction to all the fans and customers, that I sing 'Imagine what I could do to you.' I did and was surprised that no one rushed out of the store. On the contrary, it was then that I was approached by a couple of guys who turned out to be Allan Holzman and Barry Zetlin, the editor and Associate producers of a new movie that they were involved with. Linda and I were to be cast in 'Grunt' The Wrestling Movie.

We took the Kids to all the places that Linda had enjoyed most when we had Lived in Los Angeles a few years earlier. Disney Land, Universal Studios, The Basque Restaurant on 2nd Street, Santa Monica and the beachside eateries on Venice Beach. Then I hired a car and drove to Las Vegas. We stopped for a photo or two in 'Death Valley' enroute. Then we found ourselves a Hotel in Las Vegas where we stayed for a few days.

We took a trip to The Hoover Dam, and crossed over to the other side of the structure, to Arizona, just so that the Kids could say that their trip encompassed California, Nevada and Arizona. There were a number of shows we went to see. In one of them, 'The Dead Legend show, the Introducer recognized me. He briefly stopped the show to introduce me as 'World Middleweight Wrestling Champion.' He was a Welsh singer/comedian who had worked in a Club in Caerphilly in Wales, where we had Wrestled before we left the U.K. - Small World. We all admired the White Tiger in 'The Siegfried & Roy Show.' Little did we imagine, that a number of years later, it would turn on Roy and end his fantastic career.

By the time we returned to L.A. Jimmy told me that his phone had been ringing off the hook from people who wanted to meet Linda and I, or renew our acquaintance. First amongst these was 'Oingo-Boingo' who invited us all to attend their Rock-Show in a Club in Hollywood. I was delighted to accept their invitation, as Adrian and Vincent were already very much into music and were big fans of 'Oingo-Boingo'. We really got the 'Royal' treatment. We had our own private box, overlooking the stage. Then found a bottle of Champagne chilling in an ice-bucket to fortify us while we watched the show. The icing on the cake was when Oingo-Boingo hit the stage all wearing 'Exotic Adrian' T-shirts. They really knew how to put me over in front of my Kids. Backstage after the show was over we met Danny Elfman and the rest of the band.

'The Cramps' were also friends of Jimmy Maslon, and big fans of Linda and I. When they heard that we were back in town, we all got an invite to spend an evening with them in their home. It turned out that Adrian and Vince were big fans of that band also. They were thrilled when they were given some of The

Cramps music. We spent, what was for Lux and Ivy, a typical evening, by drinking wine while we watched Lux's collection of vintage striptease movies, Betty Page etc.

'The Cramps,' Poison Ivy' and Lux Interior, corresponded with serial killer John Wayne Gacey Jr. One of their most prized possessions was a picture of a Clown, painted by Gacey himself.

The night before my Kids were due to fly back to Britain, we were all sitting on Jimmy Maslon's balcony looking out over Los Angeles, eating and drinking. After everyone else had retired for the night, Vince and I decided we would attempt to see the bottom of a four litre sized bottle of red wine. It was thus armed, with a very large quantity of French/Dutch courage, that my 20 year old Son announced he had been a Father for a little over a year. 'I was now, at age 44, a wrestling Granddad, and had been for over a year already.

"Why didn't you tell me before?" I wanted to know.

"I thought you wouldn't like the idea of being a Grandfather." He replied.

I suppose I brought that one on myself, as I had always joked with my Kids about being years younger than they knew I was. I guess Vince had taken my nonsense seriously. In actual fact, I was more than delighted, I was the proud Grandfather of a one year old Boy named Gary.

Linda and I stayed on in Los Angeles for another week, and then it was time to go back to work.

BACK TO NASHVILLE

By the time we returned to Nashville, Terry Taylor, who had by now fully recovered from whatever it was that had laid him, Linda and myself low, was also back in Tennessee.

Apparently, he must have been extremely impressed by my wrestling skills during the contests he had against me for Mid South. Unbeknown to me at that time, he had been taking lessons in 'shoot wrestling' from Steve Olsonoski, aka Steve O.

Steve O, I was told, had began his pro wrestling career with the AWA after becoming a very distinguished amateur. The AWA was the promotion belonging to Verne Gagne, renowned for his shoot-wrestling ability. It was from him and some of Verne's 'real' wrestlers that Steve O learned the art of submission wrestling. Knowing that he would be wrestling against me when I returned to Tennessee from California, Terry had asked Steve O to teach him how to transform himself from prey to predator. With his newly acquired knowledge, coupled with his huge size advantage, Terry now imagined he had my number. It didn't take me too long to realize, that Terry Taylor was performing with a new found confidence - I liked that. The more aggression I experienced from an opponent the more exciting the contest. Then suddenly, Terry went for a leg dive, and as we both lay on the canvas, I became aware that he was attempting to position me for a submission hold on my left leg. It was a submission hold that I had not had applied on me since before I left Britain. I could have avoided it easily - if I had chosen to, but I was intrigued. Instead of attempting to block his attempt, I wriggled into a more accessible position - even aided his application.

'Never interrupt an enemy when they are making a mistake,' was a quote from my favorite 18th century French Emperor. It was a quote I really took to heart. I shifted myself around into a slightly more comfortable position,

"Have you got it on okay?" I asked him.

"Yeah - yeah," he chuckled.

"ARE YOU SURE?" I insisted.

"Yeah." he chuckled again, and this time he looked towards the Baby-faces dressing room and gave a big thumbs up signal in that direction. As I looked that way, I saw Steve O, with a big self satisfied grin on his chops, returning the big thumbs up signal. It was only then that the whole picture dawned on me. I asked Terry one more time,

"Are you really certain you've got it Terry?"

"Yeah - yeah." he asserted.

I twisted around, tightened my thighs and Terry Taylor squealed like a virgin on her first date with Wilt 'The Stilt' Chamberlain. I increased the pressure, as I had really enjoyed the sound and volume of Terry's squealing. Then I looked towards the Baby-Face dressing room to give Steve O my big thumbs up signal - He had disappeared?! When I saw him again, he was just a few feet away from me, standing ringside with his bottom jaw almost hanging on the ring apron, and shock registered all over his chops. He had no more idea of what had just happened to poor Terry Tailor, than poor Terry Taylor had himself.

"Get into the ring!!!" I challenged Steve O. "Challenge me to a match for next week - I dare you!!!" I implored, but he just couldn't be tempted - although I can't say I really blamed him.

For the remainder of the contest, I put Terry through the ringer. I didn't try to injure him, as I actually liked him very much. I just wanted to show Steve O, who was still standing ringside, what a wise decision he had made by not coming any closer than he was.

We knew that we were going to be in 'Grunt' The Wrestling Movie, but as yet we didn't have a firm date when we would be needed for it. In the meantime we had received an offer from 'South-Eastern Championship Wrestling.' I didn't want to start wrestling for South-Eastern Championship Wrestling until we had completed our work in 'Grunt.' I told them that as soon as we finished with the movie we would begin wrestling for them.

GULF BREEZE

We decided to phone Elizabeth, the realtor who managed our rental properties to find out if she had a vacancy for us. We would liked to have moved into the Townhouse we owned in 'The Bahama-Bay Club' as it had access to its own mini gym, a great swimming pool and was only a few minutes' walk from a 3 mile beach. Unfortunately it was already rented, but we lucked out with one of our apartments in the four-plex we owned. We found that two of our apartments were rented to two wrestlers who were already wrestling for the South-Eastern Championship Promotion. So when we moved in we found that we shared the apartments with 'The Nightmares' Kenny Wayne and Danny Davis. 'Lord Humongous', Big Boomer Lynch, 'The Flame,' Jody Hamilton, all lived within a stone's throw of my front door. Jimmy Golden, Roy Lee Welsh, Robert Fuller, Bob Armstrong, the promoter Ron Fuller all lived within a few miles.

It was quite surreal, at last living for the very first time in a property that we owned, instead of living in hotel rooms, or rental apartments all over the States. While we waited for a starting date for the movie, we walked the many white coral beaches and haunted the gyms, lifting lots of heavy weights. Life was good.

Ron Fuller, who owned South-Eastern Championship Wrestling Promotion wanted us to begin wrestling for him immediately, but I told him it would be better for us to get the movie behind us first. That way we could then give his promotion our full and undivided attention when we got back from Hollywood.

'GRUNT' THE WRESTLING MOVIE

We flew out to Los Angeles on the 8th of July 1985 to take part in the movie, most of which, would be filmed in my old 'Battle Ground' The Olympic Auditorium. I was looking forward to meeting up again with a real pair of Dicks - Dick Murdock and Dick Beyer, 'The Masked Destroyer', who played 'The Grunt Brothers. But, we found out to our disappointment, that they had already completed their roles and had left. Although I was consoled when told, that one of my songs 'Breaking Bones,' was played during their contest with 'The Mask.' 'A Mighty-Big Girl' was the background music, to our old friend 'Queen Kong' when she wrestled against Charli Haynes, 'The Golden Cat'. Last but not least 'I'm in Love with me.' introduced my old role, as compare of our own show 'Exotic Adrian's 'Street Corner.' I had only written and performed four songs at that time, and three of them were used in the movie. I decided right then that I would write and perform a lot more.

I enjoyed doing 'Street Corner' again, especially in a movie. I interviewed Bodybuilder, Bill Grant, who played wrestler 'Captain Carnage,' The Mask, played by Steve Strong with his new manager John Tollas, who played himself. I had never met John Tolos before, but we became instant friends, both enjoying the same ridiculous sense of humor. When we filmed 'Street Corner' we were only given a very rough script, and we more or less ad-libbed most of it ourselves. How John Tolos and I kept a straight face, while I continually poked him on his nose with the microphone, to emphasis my response to his comments I don't know. When I introduced their archenemy 'Captain Carnage,' my prime question began a brutal battle, which completely destroyed the set of 'Street Corner.' In the script, when the violence broke out, they had me screaming and scuttling for cover like a frantic Fairy. I had, what I thought was a much better idea. If I had adhered to the script, my action would have been completely lost in the ensuing brawl. I suggested instead, that as the fight began,

I would jump up onto my chair to call 'order', but instead of quieting everyone down, John Tolos gives me a hefty push, which lands me arse first in a trash can. Then as the battle raged, and the whole set collapsed all around us, instead of exhibiting blind panic, I give them 'The British stiff upper lip.' Although all Hell was breaking out all around me, as I sat stuck in a trash can, I turn to the camera and as cool as a cucumber announced,

"Well viewers, that ends another 'Exotic Adrian Street Corner.'

Much better, I thought, 'cos in the wild and weird World of Wrestling, Complete and utter chaos was just another day at the office.

The Battle-Royal which would decide the new champion was the spectacular climax of the film. The wrestlers taking part in the Battle Royal included, Steve Strong as 'The Mask,' Bill Grant as Captain Carnage, Michael O'Leary, Danny Spivey, Jack 'Wildman' Armstrong, Steve De Salvo, Pablo Crispin, Robert 'Rip' Merrill, Woody Farmer, Black Hawke, Steve Pardee, Black Gorman and Goliath and of course me - as myself, with Miss Linda as my Valet. It took two days to complete filming the Battle-Royal, twelve hours the first day, and twelve and a half hours on the second day. Mondo Guerrero was in the movie as a wrestler, but also got credits for the choreographer of the Battle-Royal. In fact it was me, more than he, who came up with most of the high spots of the Battle-Royal.

Danny Spivey who played 'American-Starship-Eagle' stood 6 feet 8 inches, and must have weighed about 300 pounds. I had watched him wrestle many times in the past, and had been impressed with a series of moves he used to score his victories. He would hoist his opponent high in the air, and at 6 feet 8 inches that was high. Then, instead of slamming then in the normal style, he would take a short run, leap into the air and slam his opponent without breaking contact. He would land with a resounding crash with his opponent underneath, absorbing the full force of the slam. He would then leap high into the air and finish his opponent off with a mighty leg-drop right across the unfortunate's heaving chest. I explained the move to the director, he liked my description and wanted a demonstration. BUT - it seemed that no one except me, and Danny Spivey knew how it was performed. DAMN IT!!! It was me who turned out to be the 'CRASH TEST DUMMY!!! After every one of the other wrestlers had seen it performed, none of them wanted to know. It had been my idea, and it was going to be me who was going to be the unfortunate victim. That maneuver really jarred every bone in my body and knocked the wind right out of me. As if that wasn't bad enough, I had to suffer it a dozen times for them to decide the best angles to film it from, and then a dozen more times when they actually filmed it. I got my revenge on Danny later in the match, when I ran, jumped up, caught him in a body scissors and planted a great smacking kiss on his upturned chops,

"Once again Exotic Adrian finds himself in an unnatural position!" The commentator chanted.

The Battle-Royal continued with contestant after contestant being eliminated by being hurled over the top rope.

After initially being mauled savagely by The Mad Russian, 'Commie Warhead', I came back from the dead in a way that would make Lazarus look to his laurels. I made a heroic rally, that ended when I smashed the Russian's head into the turnbuckle then kicked him right out of the ring,

"Exotic Adrian has rammed the Commie Warhead's head into the corner post. Thus freeing the World for Democracy!!!" The commentator chanted.

By now there were only three wrestlers left in the ring, Captain Carnage, The Mask and me. I decided to join forces with the Mask and help him eliminate Captain Carnage - Bad mistake! After we both gave Captain Carnage a severe beating, I hauled him up off the canvas and held both his arms behind his back for the Mask to smash him with massive forearm smashes. WHACK!!! The Mask smashes Captain Carnage so hard that he knocks him right out of my grasp, but I quickly gather him back up for the Mask to repeat the punishment. BUT - this time as he threw an even mightier blow, he purposely misses Captain Carnage, and I cop it right in the mush. I was knocked arse over tit. I leapt back to my feet and demanded that the Mask apologies for making such a clumsy for-par. The Mask immediately apologizes, and we shake on it - BAD MISTAKE! As The Mask grasps my hand he kicks me violently in the stomach, grabs both my ankles and catapults me right over the top rope. I landed right on top of the Commie Warhead's head, knocking him back where he had lain since I expelled him from the ring. Well I didn't win the Battle-Royal, but freeing the World for Democracy yet again was a fair consolation prize.

SOUTH-EASTERN CHAMPIONSHIP WRESTLING

About the same time we began wrestling for Southeastern Championship Wrestling, they changed the name of the Promotion to Continental Championship Wrestling. Both labels seemed to be interchangeable, until about 1988/90ish, when Ron Fuller sold the promotion to David Woods. David Woods owned the TV station that filmed the wrestling shows from Montgomery every week. After he obtained ownership he changed the name once more, this time to CWF - Continental Wrestling Federation.

My first contest for Southeast Championship Wrestling was a TV show held at the Boutwell Auditorium in Birmingham, Alabama. It would be against the Southeastern Heavyweight Champion, 'The Universal Heartthrob' Austin Idol.

Idol contacted Linda and I the moment we had returned from California, and he invited Linda and I to his favorite restaurant. We had first met in Tennessee, where we both enjoyed great reaction from the fans. During our meal with him and his Wife, he claimed that it was he, who had championed us, when he suggested to Ron Fuller that he should bring Linda and I into his territory as a heel opponent for himself, Austin Idol. He further suggested, that we could build up a feud situation, where I would relentlessly chase him for his Southeastern Wrestling Championship. I had different thoughts in that matter. I told him that as our first contest was to be a Southeastern Championship match, I would beat him, become the new champion, and he Austin Idol could relentlessly chase me and attempt to win it back. I found Idol to be a very smarmy git, he was completely full of shit. He had been hopping he could groom me to become his elaborate stooge. I decided otherwise.

When Linda and I arrived at The Boutwell Auditorium for our first South-Eastern Championship match, we almost collided with Austin Idol in the corridor leading from the arena's stage door. He advised us, that Linda and I could enjoy more privacy when we got ourselves changed, if we used the dressing rooms at the very top floor of the building. We took his advice and climbed a considerable number of steps to reach our objective. Idol had also told us that a steward would come and let us know when our contest was ready to commence.

After we had changed into our ring wear it seemed as though we had to wait a damn week for our contest to begin. We were Main Event, which would be the last contest of the evening, but still - I wondered just how long South-Eastern wrestling shows lasted. Eventually Linda and I went downstairs to check on the progress, and try to estimate just how much longer we would have to wait before our contest was to begin. You can just imagine what a shock we got, to find that Austin Idol was not only already in the ring, but was actually getting his hand raised in victory by the referee after he had just defeated some scrawny looking masked guy, named 'El Diablo!'

I was *#?*)#? FURIOUS!!!!! - I do like to make a BIG first impression!!! My song 'Imagine what I can do to you!' playing full blast, as Linda and I strut or stride our way to the battle ground. We would be psyching ourselves up, as we do likewise to our audience. I rushed to the ring, throwing off my heavily sequined robe in the process, I grabbed the microphone off The Master of ceremonies as I leapt through the ropes.

"HEY - WHERE DO YOU THINK YOU'RE GOING?!!!" I shouted at Idol as he was about to leave the ring.

"You should have been here ten minutes ago." he told me, "The contest is over now - you missed it!"

"I came over three thousand miles from Britain to relieve you of that Championship belt," I replied, "and you are not going anywhere until you have fought me." Idol still appeared to be anxious to leave the ring. So I continued to bait him,

"So are you going to show all your fans what a coward you are - or are you going to fight me now?!"

"You should have been here on time!" he replied lamely. I changed my tactics and instead addressed the audience,

"You fans of Austin Idol - do you regard this cowardly moron as an Idol? - Where I come from, the likes of this idiot wouldn't even make a good toilet cleaner!"

As I was still shouting at the fans, Idol made a move to step out of the ring, so I threw the microphone down and whacked him. I would have chased him all the way back to the dressing room, kicking his arse all the way if I'd had to, and he knew it. He now had no alternative - he had to stay and fight.

I could have easily beaten Austin Idol in two minutes, if I'd chosen to. He was a bodybuilder, not a wrestler. Unfortunately for him, he had pissed me off, so I punished him by extending the time it took to beat him, to just over five minutes - three more minutes of pain and humiliation. Idol got the beating he deserved and I was now the new Southeastern Heavyweight Champion, and 'The Universal Heartthrob' wasn't.

We had just one return contest, I must admit I was no gentler. For whatever reason, according to the rules in The States, you don't lose the title in a title contest on a disqualification. I was accused of striking Idol with a 'foreign object' handed to me by Linda, and as a result I was disqualified. As it happened I was falsely accused. What Linda handed me, that I used to bust the Heartthrobs chops, was a heavy roll of quarters - 'AMERICAN QUARTERS' - SEE - NOT A FOREIGN OBJECT - THEY WERE AMERICAN OBJECTS. And I was still the champion.

Now this for me was the best part of this story - although Austin Idol had made his home in Pensacola, he never wrestled for Southeastern Championship Wrestling again. The most popular wrestler in the South, Bob 'The Bullet' Armstrong, told me,

"Austin Idol is shit scared of you Adrian, he's left town and he's not coming back."

I had beaten Austin Idol - taken his title and Championship belt and driven him out of Southeastern Championship Wrestling for good - GOOD!

While still on the subject of the Southeastern Wrestling Championship Belt, I have to say it could really do with a facelift - so I gave it one. The plates were ok, but the actual leather belt was now a dirty, grimy white. Definitely not up to my standard - so I painted it bright PINK!!! It caused an uproar, as I intended it to. The Championship belt had never, ever meant so much before. Now everyone wanted to win it from me, not only to be Champion, but so that they could paint it back to its original color.

I successfully defended my Championship Belt against all comers, until I began a feud against Norvell Austin.

NORVELL

Norvell Austin was the original 'Junkyard Dog' long before Sylvester Ritter nicked that moniker. I liked Norvell and had a tremendous amount of respect for him. Like myself he was not afraid to push the envelope.

In the South, at the time Norvell became a pro wrestler, it was unusual for a black wrestler to ever step into the ring with a white wrestler. On the rare occasions that they might, they would only play the part of a heel job boy. Not only did Norvell overcome that obstacle, he became the very successful tag-team partner of 'Sputnik Monroe' a white heel wrestler. By the time we met, Norvell had earned a name for himself as an excellent fan favorite - in most of the South. Although there were a few exceptions - most notably Harlan, Kentucky.

We had wrestled each other by now, often enough to establish the fact that I was a very unpopular Champion, and everyone in the Southeastern area would have been absolutely delighted to see Norvell relieve me of the title and my 'Pink Championship Belt'. Well maybe not quite everyone in the Southeastern area.

On the journey to Harlan, Kentucky, I was told by the other wrestlers that they were really curious to witness the crowd reaction to the contest between Norvell and myself, as racial prejudice in that city was something else. They told me that on the sign post that marked the Harlan City limits, it said 'Welcome to Harlan' - then written below that was 'Do not let the sun set on your black ass!' - Linda and I obviously didn't believe a word of it. Wrestlers Worldwide are famous for coming out with the most outrageous jests, and this, we thought, was just another one of those - although not a very amusing one in my book. Just as we entered Harlan, they slowed the car to show me the famous sign post, and I found out that they had been deadly serious.

Sure enough, when we arrived at the venue, the police were there to greet us,

"I believe you have a 'Nigra' wrasslin' tonight!" they challenged.

"That is correct sir." Our promoter replied.

"What time will he be wrasslin?" the policeman demanded.

"He is in the main event, so he will be in the last contest." our promoter informed him,

"CORRECTION!" Snapped the officer - "HE WILL BE WRASSLIN' FIRST - THEN LEAVIN' TOWN!!!"

That was the way it had to be, or there would be no 'wrasslin' at all, we were told. It was well into the second half of the 80s, I would never have dreamt that that kind of attitude would be tolerated, let alone enforced.

So Norvell and I wrestled each other in the first contest that night, even though it was the main event. It really was a strange contest. The fans hated me - as they were supposed to, but they didn't seem to like Norvell much better. Response was mixed - weird, unlike any other contest we ever had. The audience was liberally sprinkled with police uniforms. As soon as the contest was over, they surrounded Norvell, escorted him back to the dressing room, where he was allowed to collect his clothes. They then escorted him out of the building. They informed us, that they would drop him off at the nearest gas station - OUTSIDE CITY LIMITS - and that we could pick him up from there, later, when the wrestling contest were over and we were all leaving town.

The attitude of the police was so unpleasant, that I decided to accompany Norvell outside the venue to where the police vehicles were parked. Most of the other wrestlers joined me. We had hardly walked more than 20 yards when a loud - CRACK-CRACK-CRACK- CRACK-CRACK!!!!! Sounded and Norvell dropped like a stone!

I thought for a second, that Norvell had been shot, but was immediately relieved when I saw him roll under a car that was parked by the side of the exit. His reflexes were quite amazing. I could smell sulfur - CRACK - CRACK - CRACK!!!!

The police have to be given top marks for their reflexes too. Guns were drawn - all assumed a firing stance.

False alarm! It turned out that some of the wrestlers, anticipating this scenario, had purchased a load of fire crackers. I did say that wrestlers were famous for coming out with outrageous jests, and this was another one of those - although, not very amusing in my book.

SHAKE WRESTLE 'N' ROLL

Shake - shake - shake wrestle 'n' roll. Shake - shake - shake
wrestle 'n' roll.
You will never feel a thing, when you're thrown around the ring,
if you shake - shake - shake wrestle 'n' roll.
I broke my old guitar 'cross someone's head,
Now I play tunes on broken ribs instead.
The double-Base and Saxophones, have been replaced by grunts
and groans.
I want you to remember what I said.
Shake - shake - shake wrestle 'n' roll. Shake - shake - shake
wrestle 'n' roll.
You will never feel a thing, when you're thrown around the ring,
If you shake - shake - shake wrestle 'n' roll.
I like breaking arms and legs and toes.
I like watching great big black eyes close.
Just remember I'm no fool, 'cos I break every single rule,
I can't help it, that's the way it goes.
Shake - shake - shake wrestle 'n' roll. Shake - shake - shake
wrestle 'n' roll,
You will never feel a thing, when you're thrown around the ring,
If you shake - shake - shake - wrestle 'n' roll.

It was about this time, inspired by the fact that 'Grunt' the
wrestling movie had contained three of the four songs that I had
written, performed and recorded, that I decided to write a
screenplay of my own. Plus I would write all the songs for the
screenplay. Shake wrestle 'n' roll,' I also decided would be the
title of the film and the title track. I carried a pen and note pads
everywhere we went to wrestle, writing - writing - writing.

After writing 'A Sweet Transvestite with a Broken Nose,' I
was asked by many of the wrestlers that we traveled with, what
kind of 'psychedelic-substance' I was flying on. I told them all
honestly, that I am a natural dope and I don't take anything mind
altering. Maybe I was inspired by what they were taking, because

there was an awful lot of sniffing and puffing going on all around us. I don't think any of my inspiration came from anything second hand, that many of the other wrestlers used and abused, but who knows? Anyway, here are the lyrics I came up with, and I promise you that the only trips I was ever on, was from home to the venue where I was wrestling, and then back home each night.

I can be a Tulip, I can be a Man,
The only way of knowing is to catch me if you can.
You can suppose what you want to suppose,
but I'm a Sweet Transvestite with a broken nose.
I've got to be Royalty, my Blood must be Blue.
I'm King of the ring, and Queen of it too.
Have you ever seen muscles on a Rose?
I'm just a Sweet Transvestite with a Broken Nose.
I'll kiss you, or I'll kick you. That's what I like the best.
I'm as tough as Marciano and as sexy as Mae West.
As cute as Shirley Temple and as fast as Bruce Lee,
I could kill a Man ----- Eventually.
I'm a poison Peacock, an Atomic Butterfly,
Better give me room, or kiss your teeth goodbye.
I hate Joan Collins, but love her taste in clothes,
I'm just a Sweet Transvestite with a Broken Nose.
I can be cruel - I can be kind.
A Butch or a Bitch - I can't make up my mind.
I can have a shave while I'm varnishing my toes.
I'm just a Sweet Transvestite with a Broken Nose.
I'll kiss you, or I'll kick you. That's what I like the best.
I'm as tough as Marciano and as sexy as Mae West.
As cute as Shirley Temple and as fast as Bruce Lee,
I could kill a Man ----- Eventually.
I love chains, leather and lace.
A Neanderthal Man with an Angel face,
Metal-studded undies and G-Strings with Bows.
I'm just a Sweet Transvestite with a Broken Nose.
If you're a he - she, or it, you'd better answer my calls.
I'm like King Kong with lipstick, Fay Wray with balls,
I wear Mink and Sable when the cold wind blows,
cos I'm a Sweet Transvestite with a Broken Nose.

TIPTOE THROUGH THE TULIPS

Before we first left Tennessee, just prior to Jerry Lawler's power play, I was going to begin a program against 'Dirty Dutch' Mantel. I had already wrestled him a few times, but in order to add some spice, they made a music video of me, to the tune of Tiny Tim's version of 'Tiptoe through the tulips.' They slowed the speed of the contest down, so that I seemed to float around the ring as light as Tinkerbelle. It really was quite amusing, and although I was supposed to be really offended, secretly I liked it. They claimed that it was 'Dirty Dutch' who had it put together, especially to piss me off. It's a shame that Dutch and I never really got into our feud. His no nonsense, macho, rough house style would have been a complete contrast to mine. Like my Archibald Cunningham, played by Tim Roth, against Dutch's Rob Roy, played by Liam Neeson, in their climatic battle in the 1995 movie 'Rob Roy.' Loved that movie.

I had a copy of the video, that Dutch had supposedly created. I thought that it would serve the same purpose that it had originally been designed for, to spice up the feud against Norvell. So I gave it to him, to show on Southeastern Championship wrestling's TV show. To set the scene, I had them show my 'Imagine what I could do to you' video, while I was standing at the podium with commentator Gordon Solie. Of course I was delighted, and praised my own performance in the video unashamedly. The next week I repeated the scenario with the video that had been made for me by Jim Crockett's promotion - 'I'm in love with me.' The scene was set for Norvell to introduce a little film of his own. When he stood next to Gordon, later on the same TV show. his introduction of 'Tiptoe through the Tulips' was a great success, Norvell, Gordon and the audience were in stitches - I was livid! - or at least pretended to be. I stormed onto the podium screaming with rage, and had to be restrained from attacking Norvell there and then. Our feud against each other just jumped to the pinnacle of the Richter scale.

Norvell vowed to take my 'Pink' Championship belt and return it to its original hue. He would almost - but not quite achieve his goal each time he tried. The only thing that prevented him, time after time, after time, was a little timely intervention by the very naughty, Miss Linda. He complained to Gordon Solie on the podium again and again,

"Gordon - I had him pinned, that title belt should now be mine - but every time I get close - that Miss Linda pokes her nose in - again and again!!!!!!!"

Norvell finally came up with the perfect solution - he would get his own Valet, to - in Norvell's own words,

"Offset that Miss Linda!"

CANDI DEVINE

Norvell's valet turned out to be the pretty, blond, Candi Devine. She would now be watching Norvell's back, in order to prevent any of Miss Linda's dastardly sneak attacks. [I have often wondered, what the fans and the police force in Harlan, Kentucky would have thought of those arrangements?!!!!!!!] Candi was a very accomplished Lady wrestler - more than a match for Miss Linda, everyone thought!

The Candi/Norvell duo worked a treat. As Linda would be about to drop a bomb on Norvell, Candi would rush to the rescue. I told Linda to avoid coming in contact with Candi at all costs. The fans imagined that Candi would pulverize the crafty Miss Linda, if she was ever to come to grips with her. I also told Candi and Norvell, that I would try at every opportunity that presented itself to get hold of Candi.

"DON'T LET THAT HAPPEN!!!" I told them. "If I can catch Candi during our contest, the fans will expect me to tear her in half. So you Candi, try not to get caught. You Norvell, if I do catch her, or even get close - you have to do whatever you can to stop me."

It made for some very exciting moments in all our contests. Sometimes I might actually get Candi cornered and get 'Pearl-Harbored by Norvell just before my drawn back fist reached its target of Candi's pretty face.

Even with Candi present to 'offset' Miss Linda, Norvell would fail by the tiniest of margins to relieve me of my Southeastern Championship Belt. That remained a vibrant, neon pink - or annoying pink, if you sympathized with the fans and my opponents.

After a few very close calls, when I 'almost' but didn't quite get beaten for the title. And almost, but didn't quite catch Candi, I announced that Norvell was no longer a contender for my title. You can never, ever fight me for my title again, I pronounced. Norvell protested, he would be the Champion he claimed. I was pressured from all sides to relent. Eventually I announced that I would give him one last shot at the Championship, but first He, with his Valet Candi Devine, would have to face me, with my Valet, Miss Linda, in a Mixed Tag-team Contest.

Both Candi and Norvell were thrilled to accept my challenge, even though they were aware that my motives were, to get closer to Candi. They were both confident in Candi's great wrestling prowess, and in the fact, that Miss Linda was just a subservient valet. She was very skilled in striking from ambush, but would fail miserably when she was met in the ring by a very skilled professional Lady wrestler.

YEAH - RIGHT!

When our contest began - everyone, and I do mean everyone, was flabbergasted when they saw Linda treat Candi the way a hungry Eagle treats a Rabbit! It was Gordon Solie who put into words, what everyone was looking at,

"I was not aware of Miss Linda's great wrestling ability - Brother, she knows her wrestling!" he gasped, "Miss Linda is a ringer - yes she's a ringer for sure. She's like Charles Bronson in the movie 'Hard Times!!!'" Linda slammed, kicked, stomped and forearm smashed Candi from pillar to ring post, and then back again. She kicked her legs, when she fell down, she kicked her head and stomped every other part of Candi's body.

Linda was a 'ringer' indeed, as Gordon Solie so concisely phrased the spectacle that was now unraveling in the ring. Linda's rampage didn't stop me from wanting to put the boot into Candi's head or ribs either, so Norvell had a fulltime job, trying to prevent me from doing just that. At one time when I was punishing Norvell with a front chokehold, Candi threw all caution to the wind, when she leapt into the ring, vaulted up onto Norvell's back and delivered a great smacking kiss right on my lips. In character, I threw an almighty fit - 'AAAAGH - KISSED BY A GIRL - HOW DISGUSTING!!!!!! I went after Candi like a jet plane - she retreated like a rocket.

Back and forth, back and forth we went. Candi managed a comeback on Linda and caught her with what Gordon Solie described as 'a low projectile dropkick.' But in no time flat Linda came back and swarmed all over poor Candi.

Norvell had his hands full 'cutting me off at the pass' time and again, just in time to prevent me from dropping the bomb I was so determined to drop on Candi. While Norvell was keeping watch on me, Linda beat on Candi. She dropped her onto the lower rope, before jumping out onto the floor, in order to achieve maximum leverage as she choked the life out of Candi, by tugging on her head, while her throat was being crushed against the bottom rope. Norvell was aghast. He rushed around the ring, grabbed Linda, picked her up bodily and carried her as far away from Candi as possible. The bad guy's tactics worked. While Norvell's attention was so effectively diverted, it was very easy for me to enter the ring. I belted poor Candi, as she still lay draped across the bottom rope. I then snatched her up and struck her in the chops, while I held her in a front face lock. Then I took her up into an almighty pile-driver. The very building seemed to shake with the force I used to bury Candi's head into the mat. As she lay prone in the centre of the ring, I leapt high into the air and landed with a great SPLASH onto Candi to score the winning pin-fall.

"I HAVE JUST LOST WHATEVER RESPECT I MIGHT HAVE HAD FOR THE EXOTIC ADRIAN STREET!!!!" Gordon Solie screamed into his microphone, as the fans screamed the roof off Boutwell Auditorium. "We have an injured young Lady in Candi Devine!" he added.

This defeat did nothing to diminish Norvell's determination to win my championship belt, if anything it made him even more determined to beat me. He decided it was time to bring out the BIG GUNS!

MAD MAXINE

Next, Norvell brought in 'Mad Maxine' as his personal bodyguard, and promised that she would succeed, where Candi Devine had failed to keep Linda at bay. The promotion billed her as being 6' 6" tall. Now whether that was to the top of her head, or to the top of her Mohican hairdo, I don't know. Either way, she was a mighty big girl for her age.

Maxine had been trained by one of the toughest Lady wrestlers, ever to don a leotard, The Fabulous Moolah. Moolah was wrestling for the WWF at that time, and that was where Mad Maxine had made her debut. The Giant Maxine was obviously influenced by the 'Mad Max' movies. To enhance her ring persona, she wore a full Road Warrior outfit, which resembled those worn in the movie to a T. The first time I saw, or heard of her was during a TV interview, in which she warned Linda of her pending arrival, and the treatment that Linda could expect when she did.

"Seems like that Miss Linda keeps cropping up like bad food," she exclaimed, "My good friend Candi Devine couldn't get the job done, but Miss Linda will not get past me. And you Exotic Adrian - if you get in the way - the same thing could happen to you!" Maxine emphasized her last statement, by waving a fist at the camera that appeared to be roughly twice the size of my own fist - OOOOPS!!!

The first time the fans saw 'Lady' Maxine, as she now called herself, stride to the ring beside Norvell, they all gasped. She towered over him. I gasped myself - she looked like Lurch's big Sister.

I did not want a repetition of 'The Norvell/Candi Devine saga,' So, instead of me chasing after Norvell's Female confederate, intent on ultimate destruction, I completely reversed our roles. This time Norvell's giant assistant would be the predator, Linda and I would be the prey. If she so much as made one hostile step towards us, we would take a number of rapid steps back. If she got too close, playing the cowardly heel, I would even step quickly behind Linda, suggesting that I would not hesitate in sacrificing her safety in order to protect my own. We soon had all Norvell's fans believing what we wanted them to believe - that Linda and I both, were terrified of Norvell Austin's Giant Lady Bodyguard.

From the very beginning, each time Linda made the slightest hostile move towards Norvell, in order to help me out of yet another sticky situation, much to the fan's delight, Giant Lady Maxine would be right in her face. But, in spite of Lady Maxine's constant timely intervention, the prize, namely The Southeastern Championship Belt still eluded Norvell. So, in spite of The Giantess's disturbing presence, I still managed to cling to the Pink wrestling belt. BUT, one night that all changed. I was so distracted on this occasion, as I had Norvell, literally on the ropes pummeling again - again and again with a series of mighty over arm smashes down onto his upper chest and throat. I was so intent on maximizing the punishment, that I was unaware of Lady Lurch leaping to the rescue. As I was hurling forearms with all my might, my face was suddenly clamped in a vice like grip. It was The Giantess, who held me with her hands either side of my face, as she stood outside the ring on the ring apron. She easily reached right over Norvell who was still draped across the ropes and planted a huge GIANT sized kiss right on my pretty chops. I was so infuriated - being kissed by a huge female, I threw caution to the wind and attempted to Strike her right off the ring apron. However, Giant Lady Maxine beat me to the punch - and WHAT A PUNCH! I was lifted a yard off the canvas and landed flat on my back in the middle of the ring. Then the mighty Giantess almost lifted Norvell bodily as she hurled him after me. SPLAT!!! Norvell landed right on top of me - three seconds later he rose to his feet with the help of Maxine, and was at last awarded the prize that had alluded him for so very long. Norvell Austin was now the new 'Southeastern Wrestling Champion. The Pink Belt would at last be repainted white.

As soon as I recovered my wits and composure, I wasted no time in challenging Norvell to a rematch. In fact, I was still standing in the middle of the ring, screaming into the microphone that I had snatched out of the hands of the M.C. By this time Norvell was on the podium and standing next to Gordon Solie, who pushed his own microphone towards Norvell, so that he could respond to my challenge. First Norvell reminded me of the stipulations that I had made, in order to make things more difficult for him when he had challenged me.

"As the new Champion, I have a stipulation of my own." he added, "I am now naming my own number one contender. A contender, that you have to defeat before I give you a chance to fight me for the title ----"

"I'LL FIGHT ANYONE!!!" I interrupted, "I WANT MY TITLE BACK - I DON'T WANT YOUR GRUBBY HANDS TO EVEN TOUCH IT!!!"

"Okay," Norvell replied, "in order to earn another chance at the title, you have to defeat my number one contender - THE LADY GIANT MAXINE!!!"

"WHAT ARE YOU TALKING ABOUT?!" I screamed, "I WON'T FIGHT A WOMAN - WHO DO YOU THINK I AM - ANDY KAUFMAN?!"

"What about Candi Devine?! Norvell hollered back, "You didn't mind wrestling with her!"

"I WILL NEVER GET IN THE RING WITH THAT OVERGROWN AMAZON!!!" I stated, but Norvell was now the champion, he had my Championship Belt. It was agree to his stipulation or never get the chance to win it back. Everyone was enjoying my discomfort immensely. They were convinced that when Mad Maxine got me in the ring, one on one, that she was capable of completely annihilating me. The fear I had shown every time Maxine got close, the mighty punch she had delivered that sent me flying backwards across the ring, where I fell easy prey for Norvell's winning pin-fall.

If there was one person, who believed more than anyone else, that Mad Maxine could beat me, it was Mad Maxine herself. I secretly congratulated myself on a job well done. The scene was set, everyone, especially Mad Maxine thought that she would win our battle.

I had to enter the ring alone - stipulations also declared that Miss Linda would be banned from ringside. That in everyone's mind robbed me of my only chance of coming out of this dreadful conflict in one piece. The applause Maxine received from the fans was roof shattering, they couldn't wait to watch her go to work. The fans pent up anticipation was palatable, any second now they would witness my utter demise. How would I ever be able to hold my head up again,

"YOU GOT BEAT BY A GIRL!!!!!!!!" They would never tire of reminding me.

Maxine attacked - but I ducked, dived and retreated. 'Soon' they all thought - soon, I'd get caught and get my comeuppance, plus a healthy bonus. Maxine's giant fist whizzed past my face for the umpteenth time, just missing by a fraction of an inch. I ducked, dived and retreated. Suddenly I grabbed her arm and sent her flying into one of the corner posts. I just hesitated long enough for her to anticipate what I intended to do next. Then took off at breakneck speed, as though I intended to crush her against the ring post with the full weight of my body. Just as I anticipated, it just gave her time to meet my headlong charge with high kick from one giant boot. - IT NEARLY TOOK MY BLOODY HEAD OFF!!! As I struggled to get back to my feet, the crowd roared like thunder as Maxine followed her advantage with a series of punches that rocked my World.

"OUCH!!!!!" That's enough of that CRAP!!!! I changed gear and threw the giant Lady Maxine all around the ring as though she was a giant rag-doll. I took just a little time, to show her what wrestling was all about, before I lowered the boom!!! The deafening roar of the crowd was reduced to a whimper. Then I picked the giantess up, slammed her down then launched myself into the air. I did a high flying elbow-drop with a twist. As I crashed down on her I purposely drove my elbow right into her crotch. The ringside TV camera man almost fell over, trying NOT to film what I had done. For a second you could hear a pin drop. Even Gordon Solie was rendered speechless. Then the boos hit a crescendo, as The Giant Lady Maxine was carried from the ring.

I had earned my return Southeastern Championship contest against Norvell Austin. With a little help from my reinstated Valet, I regained it, and returned it once more to a vivid pink. I refused his challenge to a rematch. My feud against Norvell Austin had ran its course - it was time to move on.

A WILDCAT NAMED GWENDOLYN

One of the best feuds we were to engage in wasn't really meant to be. Wendall Cooley was just supposed to be a temporary opponent. They intended just using him as a job-boy. Although he had been born and raised in the Southeastern area, he hadn't yet wrestled there. He debuted in Texas, and had wrestled as Rick Casey, fictitious cousin of my old Texas adversary, Scott Casey. In Texas the Casey Cousins had enjoyed regular Main Event status, but here for Southeastern Championship Wrestling, his role was to be no more than a temporary knockoff. Our contests were brutal and exciting. Not only were their impact an immediate crowd magnet, but they added a great deal to both Wendall's and my legacy.

From our very first encounter, I saw far more potential than our promotion had in mind for him. First and foremost, the fans loved him. He was 6 feet tall and weighed in at a trim but muscular 235 pounds. He was good looking and Country through and through - I called him Gwendolyn Cuddly. When I had feuded with Norvell, in order to appear to be really upset with him, I had given him a music video, that I had pretended to be offended by. I needed an angle to promote some serious heat. In my next televised contest against The Wildcat, I pulled out all stops. If I wasn't pummeling him from all angles myself, I was busy distracting the referee while Linda was getting in one devastating cheap shot after another. Between us we beat Wendall black and blue. Eventually he made a terrific comeback, it looked as though he may have stood a chance after all. He caught me in a full-nelson and battered my head into the corner post. Once again he repeated this devastating maneuver. HA-HA! It was not to be, I spun out of his powerful hold, and as I catapulted myself behind him, I leapt up and scissored his right arm with both of my legs. The weight and impetus of my body tore the Wildcat off his feet onto the canvas, where I twisted him into my 'special unbreakable pin-fall.'

"ONE - TWO!!!" Shouted the referee, as I forced Wenall's shoulders into the canvas. Then there was an explosion, as The Wildcat burst free and reversed my pin-fall into one of his own. The Wildcat was now the new Champion. No sooner did he have his hand raised in victory by the referee, than he grabbed the coveted Championship belt, rushed out of the ring and up onto the podium to join Gordon Solie. There he could gloat and rub a little more salt into my wounded pride. I responded by claiming that everyone present and at home watching on television, had just witnessed the biggest fluke in wrestling history. I had wrested all over the World and won championship after championship everywhere I had appeared, by using the same hold that Cooley had just broken out of, and reversed in order to score his victory. It was such a fluke, that I refused to accept the verdict, and he should return at once to the ring in order to finish the contest, that I claimed had hardly began. He repeated what I had told him to say before we entered the ring, 'that he was the one and only wrestler in the World to ever break out of my unbreakable hold'. I immediately demanded a rematch in order to regain my Pink Championship belt, before The Wildcat had time to restore it to its original white color.

"I am painting it white!!!" he promised, "and if you want a rematch, I'll give you one. "BUT - there is a condition. If you lose the rematch, you also lose Miss Linda and she will become my valet." I agreed immediately, suggesting that the Continental Championship Title meant more to me that Miss Linda did.

Well we had our contest, and I lost that too, and I also lost Miss Linda, she was now Wendall's valet.

Now this gets a little complicated, so bear with me.

A televised contest would be aired in different areas at different times. In the Birmingham area they might see it a certain time, down south it may be a week earlier or later. So even though the fans in one area thought that Linda was now The Wildcat's valet, in another area she was still mine. They wouldn't be aware of the angle, where I lost Linda for as much as a week or so after they saw it on TV.

It was at a venue where Linda and I was still together, that Linda slipped and fell down a slippery slope outside the arena, as we were leaving. I remember telling to get up before anyone saw her sitting at the bottom of the slope, as I didn't want any of the fans to have a laugh at our expense. I didn't realize that Linda was really very badly injured. I grabbed up the bag containing Linda's wrestling wear and expected Linda to quickly get up and follow me to our van. As I threw our bags into the van, I turned and saw Linda was still sitting on the ground, almost a hundred yards away. I swore and went back to help her up, but she could not get to her feet. I had to pick her up bodily, and carry her to the van. It was only then, that I began to realize how badly injured she was. I wanted to take her to the nearest Hospital, but Linda insisted that she wanted to go to the Hospital near our home in Gulf Breeze - over 300 miles away. Linda is tough, but the poor Girl was in agony, all the way back to Florida. It was in the early hours of the next morning when we arrived at the Hospital. Gulf Breeze Hospital was brand new at that time and the best they could do was to put a support on her ankle and told us to go to Baptist Hospital in Pensacola. I drove Linda there myself, and after she was admitted, she was X-Rayed to find that she had a broken ankle and a torn ligament. She had to have three metal pins implanted into the bones of her ankle, and was encased in plaster from her foot to just below her knee.

Nevertheless, as they say, the show must go on, and Linda was the major player in the hottest angle in Continental at that time. BUT!!!!! - in some areas they were only just seeing the angle on TV, where I had just lost Linda to Wendall Cooley. To make matters more complicated she hadn't been injured then, and had been very, very active during that contest. She had been sticking the boot, of her now injured ankle, into poor Wendall every possible opportunity that presented itself during that contest. This was not something that could be disguised - Linda was injured, with a plaster cast on her leg, and only able to hobble about on crutches.

The best they could do, was to come up with a storyline that I absolutely hated. Their story was, that as my Valet, Linda, had never been exposed to any outdoorsy type of activity whatsoever. In order to introduce her to the Cowboy way of life, she had been ordered to mount a Horse. A Horse that she had proved unable to handle. She had been thrown off, and had subsequently received her injuries as a result. I was genuinely pissed off. Both Linda and I, were extremely proud of her equine prowess. In my opinion, Linda had forgotten more about Horse ridding, than most of those Hee-Haw rejects had learned in a lifetime. I described in one of my previous books, how Linda had taught Horse riding from her mid teens, including teaching Michael Cain to ride a Horse for his role in the movie 'Zulu.' I do think that our total disgust, may have contributed to increasing our aggression in the ring from that point on.

I was now one hundred-percent focused on recovering both my title and my Valet. In a contest which was for the return of Miss Linda - if I won, I won. Actually Miss Linda won herself back to my side. Just when it looked as though The Wildcat was going to get a pin-fall, after nailing me with an avalanche of unrestrained violence, Linda made her move. The referee's count had reached two, when Linda leaned into the ring and used her crutch in a massive uppercut that all but decapitated Gwendolyn. I rolled over on him and this time the referee's count reached the magic THREE! Linda was once more my Valet.

From the podium Gwendolyn Cuddly vowed to both Gordon Solie, the fans in the arena and all those watching their TV screens, that next time he was going to give me everything he thought I deserved,

"I'm going the send the Exotic Adrian Street down the road of humiliation further than any man has ever been." he stated.

Next time The Wildcat appeared on the podium next to Gordon, he was accompanied by 'Miss Eli Mae Spicket.' Eli Mae was a figurine manufactured out of a lady's wig that surmounted a dummy face, atop PVC pipe frame. She wore a dress that he demanded, I would have to wear, if I lost the contest.

So Wildcat Wendall Cooley wanted to see me wearing a Lady's dress, and the closest he could come, to obtaining a valet of his own, was to manufacture one out of PVC Pipe and dress her in a cheap, gaudy, garish gown.

"There's definitely something very strange about this Cowboy." I declared.

The Wildcat entered the ring first, amid huge cheers, as his music blared away - 'If Heaven ain't a lot like Dixie.' He approached the ring carrying his Lady valet 'Miss Eli Mae

Spicket' with him. He stood her ringside, so that she could get a good view of her hero in action. She was wearing the very colorful dress, that Gwendolyn swore I would be wearing before the night had ended. The closet case Cowboy, stomped impatiently around the ring, as the loud blast from the loudspeakers 'Imagine what I could do to you', announced the entrance of Miss Linda and myself.

Wendall was so wired up, that I was unable to enter the ring to disrobe. After several attempts, I threw my beautiful shimmering Gold and Black gown to Linda and tried once more to climb into our battleground. The Wildcat exploded out of the ring and attacked - even Miss Eli Mae Spicket took a bump onto the arena's concrete floor. I was pummeled from backside to breakfast time, before being hurled into the ring and pummeled some more. Apart from what mostly amounted to a small amount of ineffectual retaliation from myself, I was beaten upside-down - inside-out, both in and out of The Ladies chamber. I was caught with 'The Texas Lariat' then the devastating 'Oklahoma Bulldog' before being rolled over onto my shoulders for that dreaded three-count.

I had lost - The Wildcat had won - now it was dressing up time. Wendall leapt from the ring - stripped Eli Mae Spicket of her gaudy garments - then leapt back into the ring to complete his victory. As he lifted my head off the canvas in order to slip the dress over it, all Gwendolyn's lights went out. Linda had charged into the ring. Now brandishing her crutch, as Richard the Lionhearted would brandish his battleaxe, she brought it down with all her might. WOW! She almost decapitated the Wildcat. After rolling him off me, Linda set about reviving me. Then we both got set to dress Gwendolyn up, in Eli Mae Spicket's dress. Then in order to complete his sexy ensemble, we daubed the crucified Cowboy with our brightest eye makeup and scarlet lipstick. We then left him to find his own way back to consciousness, as we made our way up to join Gordon Solie at the podium. Linda and I were still giggling girlishly, when Gwendolyn awoke and found himself in drag. The ensuing Wardance along with his garish makeup made him appear more like an Indian than a Cowboy. I grabbed the microphone from Gordon,

"Didn't I tell you 'There's something very strange about a Cowboy,' Gordon?! - then to Gwendolyn I crooned, "OH, YOU SWEET THING - YOU LOOK SO CUTE IN THAT DRESS!!!" It took him no time flat, to agree to once more put the Continental title back on the table, if only to get me back into the ring, and get his revenge.

What did he say about traveling down the road of humiliation?!

'SHAKE WRESTLE 'N' ROLL'

Shake, shake, shake, wrestle 'n' roll - shake, shake, shake, wrestle
'n' roll.
You will never feel a thing, when you're thrown around the ring,
if you shake, shake, shake, wrestle 'n' roll.
I broke my old guitar 'cross someone's head.
Now I play tunes on broken ribs instead.
The double base and saxophones have been replaced by grunts
and groans.
I want you to remember what I said.
I like breaking arms and legs and toes. I like watching great big
black eyes close.
Let me tell you, I'm no fool. Cos' I break every single rule.
I can't help it, that's the way it goes.

I had written eight more songs to add to the four I already
had. Time to put an album together, and my music man, Don
Woods, would be flying out with the music tracks he had written
for my lyrics. It crossed my mind, that history was repeating
itself. At the time that I first met Don in Britain, and we had
recorded my first single record, I was on crutches after tearing
my Achilles Tendon in half. Now, when we met again to record
my first album, Linda was on crutches.

He had advised me to book a recording studio in advance. I
managed to find one in Pensacola, but was quoted a fee for its
use, that was extortionate to put it mildly. Added to that, they told
me that for that price, I would only be able to rent the studio for a
couple of hours and not a second longer. I do not like time limits.
I didn't like the fee either. Time to put on the thinking cap.

In Mobile there was a Radio Station WABB where I had
previously done a few interviews. I had been taken to the studio
originally by TV Newscaster, Ron Goldnik. The radio station
DJ's name was Dennis Stacey, but used to be known as 'Hound
Dawg' when he did his thing on the air. I phoned Dennis and told
him of my predicament,

"Come and make your album here, Adrian," he invited, "you can spend as much time as it takes." Now that was much better, and it wasn't going to cost me a dime. The extra advantage of that deal was, that as Hound Dawg was the DJ, he would be likely to play our music on the radio - GREAT PUBLICITY. Well instead of having to suffer the aggravation of the overly expensive Pensacola studio, Linda, Don, Hound Dog and I had a ball. We really enjoyed our session - making sweet music. Well - maybe not exactly sweet, but as close as I could come. 'Shake Wrestle 'n' roll' was now a 12 track album - BUT - I hadn't finished with Don Woods yet!!!! "You'll come handy watching Linda's back." I told him.

"YEAH - AND WHO'S GOING TO WATCH MINE?!!!!! He complained. Nevertheless, I dressed Don up in some 'Exotic' Clobber, and he became my unbearably British Barrister/come Manager. We named him Sir Cedric Everard Hathaway - he particularly liked the Everard bit, which he always pronounced 'ever hard.'

This is a word for word letter I just received from Don, when I told him, that I had began writing about his time with Linda and I in Continental Championship Wrestling.

'Hi Ade. Be careful what you put in that book about Sir Cedric - his barristers are on high alert. I remember being extremely jet lagged when I arrived in Birmingham, Alabama, and you forced me into those bloody tights and gay top, and made me go out into the crowd. I wore sunglasses to disguise the fear. Then some hick came running up and called me a fucking homo - to which you strolled over and said,

"Why don't you go away and have a wank?" which didn't help the situation. We went up to Gordon Solie and you said,

"I had a rough night last night Gordon - and speaking of rough nights, this is Sir Cedric Everard Hathaway - my barrister from London." Gordon was trying not to crack up. I then had to give my judgment on a wrestling match I hadn't even seen. So I looked at a small screen, to see Linda nearly take Wendall Cooley's head off with her crutch,

"No case to answer," I haughtily replied, "he tried to grab the crutch and hit himself with it." - Which went down really well - I remember thinking after all I've done, what a place to finally go.

A few days later, you were fighting Wendall again, and you told me to sneak around the ring menacingly. When Wendall saw me, he jumped over the top rope and my immediate thoughts were,

'I hope he knows I don't fucking wrestle.' With visions of him pile-driving me into the concrete - which wouldn't have been good with my lack of knowledge - so I was OFF!!!

Then I had to sit in your place on Saturday night and watch what a cunt I was, with you guffawing - But I've since forgiven you.

Great memories,

catch you buddy, love to the Babe,

Don'

' Sir Cedric was happy enough conducting interviews with Gordon Solie at the podium on stage, but there was no way he could be induced to again stand in THE DANGER ZONE, ringside, with poor crippled Linda.

MY 'ROYAL PINK' WRESTLING BELT

Sir Cedric posed as my Manager and Barrister, any rules were hotly contested by him, if they were in any way contrary to our way of thinking. He would dispute any 'American' rules with Gordon Solie, while standing with him at the podium. If Gordon pointed out that in America, American rules were indeed valid, Sir Cedric's response would be,

"Now be very careful Mr. Solie - as you know, I have a lot of pull in England, and you could be attending your last garden party with her Majesty - mark my words Mr. Solie. You have been warned."

Sir Cedric's continual reference, to his intimate connections to Britain's Royal family, gave my an idea.

Since first winning the Continental Championship, and then painting the belt bright pink, I had lost it, first to Norvell Austin and then a couple of times to Wendall Cooley. Both had repainted it back to its original white color. Each time I had regained it, I had wasted no time repainting it pink. By now the symbol of Continental's supreme Champion was in very, very poor condition - But, Sir Cedric's ranting had given me this outrageous idea.

I made an outrageous PINK CHAMPIONSHIP WRESTLING BELT MYSELF - WITH A PHOTO OF MYSELF ON THE BELT'S MAIN PLATE! Then I claimed, that it had been designed and commissioned for me by Britain's Royal family. It turned out to be an instant success, it totally eclipsed the sorry piece of crap that had symbolized Continental Championship's highest honor for so long.

BUT! Almost immediately, I received a very negative - even hostile response from Continental's management. They decided that the next time I stood on the podium with Gordon Solie, showing off the new belt and boasting about it, I would be attacked by Wendall, who would completely destroy it,

"That way everyone will know that it isn't a real championship belt." they explained. I absolutely refused to go along with this stupid idea. I knew that they were upset because my belt put the legitimate Championship belt in the shade. But that had been my motive in the first place. They even offered to pay me, if I would agree to their ridiculous plan.

"If anyone comes close to me while I'm showing off my Royal Pink Wrestling Belt," I warned, "it will be them who gets destroyed, not my belt!"

A number of years later, I was even more pleased that I didn't adhere to their idiocy - when I sold the belt to a collector for a couple of thousand dollars.

The next time Linda and I faced the Wildcat, all HELL broke loose. That's okay if that occurs in the ring, but this time it was ringside. In spite of the fact that I had purposely decided, that for this contest, Linda was not really going to get involved on account of her broken ankle, she still posed a threat in the fan's minds. I had been on the receiving end of a severe thrashing, and in order to keep the fans on their toes, I just looked at Linda and gave her a nod of my head. As it happened, neither Linda and I intend doing anything underhand at that particular time - we would sometimes do it just to aggravate. But no sooner did Linda return my sly nod, than a screaming Woman rushed out of the audience, and launched herself up in the air and crash landed right on top of Linda. Linda was bowled right off her crutches by this bloody Wild woman. Wendall had been in the process of attacking me, but when I saw the crippled Linda being smashed completely off her crutches, I just brushed him aside and leapt out of the ring. As devastating as the attack looked, the Lady thug had made a mistake taking a crippled Amazon to the ground. She had a good hold on Linda's hair, but Linda was now on top, smashing her repeatedly in the face alternatively with both fists. By the time I grabbed them, in order to pries them apart, a half dozen Police officers were right there with the same thought in mind. Between us we must have dragged Linda and her attacker half way around the ring before they were finally separated. I looked down and saw a trail of blood from the spot where Linda had been attacked, right up the where the Police and I finally pulled them apart. A quick check of Linda showed that it was not her bleeding. I looked at her attacker as the Police dragged her away - she was covered in blood - completely scarlet. The Police took the Woman away, where she spent the night in a cell, while Linda and I carried on with our contest. I went on to defeat the Wildcat and once more regain MY Championship belt that once again became much more colorful.

Nevertheless, I was upset to think that someone would attack Linda, especially as she was only able to get about on crutches. I don't like being attacked by fans myself, but in my case, I can usually see it coming. But while I enjoy the safety of being inside the ring, poor Linda is unprotected on the outside - with her back to the enemy, while she's watching the action in the ring and standing right in THE DANGER ZONE.

THE BADEST OF THE BAD, BECOMES THE GOODESST OF THE GOOD

TV sportscaster Ron Goldnik had been trying for days to track down Linda and I. We were on the road traveling from town to town, wrestling each night in a different venue, and staying each night in a different motel. By the time he finally managed to make contact, his quest had become quite dire. He took little time in explaining. He told us, that he had been contacted by a Hospital in Mobile. They, knowing that he was a friend of Linda and I, had asked him to help contact us, with a very special request. He told us that there was a little Girl in the Hospital, who was suffering with Cystic-fibrosis. By the time Ron had managed to contact us, her Doctor had given her just 48 hours to live. Her dying wish was to meet Linda and I. When Ron had found that he might be running out of time, trying to contact Linda and I, he had asked the little girl, if Magic Johnson might substitute for us.

"Who's Magic Johnson?" was her response.

When Linda and I arrived at the hospital, we brought with us whatever little presents we thought that the young Girl, whose name was Lisa Rush might enjoy. Signed photos, Exotic Adrian and Miss Linda T-shirts and such. I think little Lisa was about 13 to 14 years old at that time, but when I gave her a hug, I couldn't believe that she could have been any more than 8 or 9, she seemed to be a weightless bag of tiny bones. She was a lovely child, it was heartbreaking to see her that way. As we chatted to her, her replies came in little pants and gasps, but both Linda and I really began to feel that our presence had really cheered little Lisa up.

"Okay," I told her, "Miss Linda and I have come to see you, now you have to do something for us. I have Miss Linda as my Valet, but now Miss Linda needs a Valet too. What we want you to do, is to get better as soon as you can. Then, when ever Miss

Linda and I are wrestling anywhere near Mobile, your parents can bring you to the show and we will have a special 'Exotic' gown for you to wear when you come to the ring with us. Would you like that?" I asked.

"Oh yes, I would." she replied.

"Okay - promise Miss Linda and I, that you are going to start getting better right away." I told her. She promised she would.

Linda and I phoned Lisa every day. We were given a report on her progress at the same time. She seemed to be doing better - some of those dreadful plastic tubes had been removed - she had been allowed out into the Hospital grounds in a wheelchair - she had been allowed outside in the Hospital grounds without a wheel chair. They even began calling her primary Physician 'Exotic Dr. Bob.' Finally they let her go home. Eventually she even began taking up Ballet.

True to her word, little Lisa Rush began attending all the venues in her area where she became 'special' Valet to Miss Linda and I. During this period, Ron Goldnik and his TV camera crew had been recording Lisa's progress - it really cast 'The Merchant of Menace' in a much more benevolent role.

Under normal circumstances, I would have been horrified, as this whole scenario made Linda and I look human, instead of the heartless villains we had always appeared to be. I must admit, that I had always preferred to play the villain, but after that episode when Linda was attacked, when she was hardly unable to walk, made me rethink. Maybe it was time for a change.

In the Mobile area of Continental Championship Wrestling Linda and I went from being 'public enemy number one and two,' to the most loved duo ever - all on account of little Lisa Rush. Up north in all of the other areas of Continental, it was only a matter of weeks before the whole story spread. On the very next TV show in Birmingham I seized an opportunity to accelerate its progress.

Continental's ultimate hero at that time was 'The Bullet'.

'The Bullet' Bob Armstrong was well and truly engaged in a very hot and heavy conflict with 'The Stud Stable.' A motley crew of villains that comprised of Robert Fuller, Jimmy Golden and Tom Pritchard. On this night 'The Masked Bullet' was having a rousing contest against some other villain, when the whole Stud

Stable, reinforced by a small hoard of villainous confederates invaded the ring and began dismantling the very popular masked vigilante. Seeing this occur, I also saw an opportunity to jet propel the inevitable. I took off - after leaping of the stage, I charged into the ring as fast as my feet would carry me. At first I was greeted with boos from the fans, who understandably imagined that I too intended to attack the Bullet. It wasn't until I began to rip into The Bullet's attackers with devastating violence, that the astonished fans cheered me like never before. Well actually - they never had cheered me before - period. Fighting back to back, the Bullet and I cleared the ring of The Stud Stable and all their criminal confederates. In a matter of minutes Bullet Bob Armstrong and the Exotic Adrian Street became the hottest 'GOOD GUYS' in Continental Championship Wrestling. BUT! Gaining a friend in Bullet Bob also gained a host of enemies in The Stud's Stable. They wasted no time in attempting to exact some violent revenge, for the unwanted interference I had meted out against them, on behalf of The Bullet.

On my very next contest in that arena, I was engaged for the very first time wrestling as a good guy against a heel. The contest had hardly time to progress before the ring was once more invaded by The Stud Stable, reinforced by every other bad guy on the card. Revenge was on their mind. I was to be taught that they would not tolerate interference. I was attacked from all sides, but battled back at them like a nasty little Wolverine. Before they really gained any advantage at all, they were thwarted by the Cavalry. 'Bullet Bob' Armstrong hit the ring and then proceeded to hit everything in it. Everything that is except me. Between the Bullet and I, we cleared the ring, amid thunderous applause from all the fans in that packed arena. Bullet Bob and I became regular tag-team partners, feuding mostly against The Stud's Stable.

It was about this time that Continental expanded its territory, and as a result recruited very many more wrestlers in order to fill the extra venues. Chattanooga and Knoxville in the north became regular venues, plus many spot shows in that area. Linda and I decided to rent an apartment in Birmingham as traveling from the Knoxville area all the way home to Gulf Breeze was a journey of over 500 miles each way.

Amongst the new recruits was our very good friends, Nancy and Kevin Sullivan. They also rented an apartment in the building right next to ours. We had so many delicious meals together. Sometimes Linda or I would cook, other times it would be Nancy. She too was an excellent cook. These were times we will always remember.

Kevin had been a booker/matchmaker in Knoxville for a number of years before. He predicted that the fans in Knoxville would never, ever, accept Linda and I as Babyfaces, but they did - I mean - they really did.

HAWAII

Kevin had kept in touch with Mark Lewin, who had been his 'Purple Haze' and now lived in Honolulu, Hawaii. Both Mark and Rocky Johnson wrestled for Leah Maivia, Wife of my old friend Peter Maivia. Unfortunately, Peter had died a few years earlier. Rocky Johnson had married Peter's Daughter, who I hadn't seen since she and her Mum and Dad, lived just around the corner from me in London in 1962.

We flew to Hawaii with Kevin and Nancy. The first night I wrestled was against Dusty Wolfe, Linda wrestled against Debbie combs. We both had excellent contests against great opponents. The tour was more like a holiday than work. Our hotel room overlooked Waikiki Beach and the vast Pacific Ocean. Over to our left as we faced the beach, we had a great view of Diamondhead. We didn't wrestle every night, and even on the nights we did, we would always have all day to ourselves. We wrestled on all the islands except the privately owned one, and all the other islands were only a short flight away. If we flew from Honolulu early, we would have all day to explore a new island before wrestling at night. If we left late, we would spend most of the day doing what we wanted to do in Honolulu. A typical day would be Breakfast, an hour or so in the Sun, then we would window-shop our way to Gold's Gym. There we would often join Mark Lewin and Rocky Johnson for a couple of hours workout.

On one occasion while Linda and I were training alone, we were approached by a young man who waited patiently until I'd finished my set, then addressed me in a pleasant soft spoken voice,

"Excuse me sir, but I believe you know my Father." I was very impressed by this young man's politeness, I was also impressed by the size of this young 14 year old Kid. He stood 6 feet 2 inches and weighed 225 pounds at the age of 14.

"If you are who I think you are," I replied, I do know your Father, and I also knew your Grandfather, Peter Maivia even better. We were neighbors in London over 20 years ago. Both he and I had been correct, the young man was Dwayne Johnson, who would become 'The Rock,' one of the most magnificent physical specimens I have ever seen.

Whilst strolling on Waikiki Beach we bumped into The Giant King Curtis Laukea. I hadn't seen him since the mid 60s - that was on the night he'd got his head split open by a very clumsy Andy Robbins in Scotland. We chatted for hours. He described himself as a Beach bum, who occasionally came out of retirement and wrestled, if the price was right.

We also made friends with some of the local wrestlers who would take all of us imports to all the places of interest in Honolulu. We saw some beautiful and magnificent sights, smoking volcanoes, fantastic waterfalls and a number of native villages. Our first Hawaiian tour was Towards the end of 1986 - we made a number of return trips during the first half of 1987.

****

Randy Savage and Jimmy Hart phoned me to tell me that they had been working in Pensacola for the WWF. They had called earlier, but we had only just returned home ourselves minutes before, from a venue where I had been wrestling.

"Yes, I told them, "I could pick them up and give them a bed for the night." By this time, they had already got a cab to drop them off at a Supermarket, not far from where we lived. Linda and I were not prepared for the sight that awaited us when we arrived. The Macho-man was laying flat on his back with arms outstretched and Jimmy Hart was asleep in a shopping cart. They were both absolutely exhausted. When they could, they explained that they had been flying from one venue after another, and hadn't had a good night's sleep for more than a week. In our spare bedroom, Linda and I had set up a little gym, with plenty of heavy weights. When Randy was ready for bed I showed it to him and told him he was welcome to have himself a good workout the next morning.

"I'm sure those weights will be heavy enough for you." I told him.

"Yeah," he yawned, "If they leave me alone - I'll leave them alone!" I think he was asleep before I closed the bedroom door.

Jimmy Hart told me that Vince McMahon had decided there was room in pro wrestling for yet another 'Exotic Adrian' doppelganger and Jimmy Hart was going to be his/her manager. He also told me, that when I first wrestled in Tennessee, he had been so amused by the innuendos I had used during my interviews, he had written them all down, and they would now be used for Vince's new 'Exotic' creation.

Enter 'Adorable' Adrian Adonis. Out of a mild interest, I watched him make his debut. It came in the form of an announcement that he was going to 'come out of the closet' and that he was gay. I knew at once that 'Queen' or not, he had Royally fucked up. The very thing that made my gimmick work, was the mystery involved - is he, or isn't he????? My peculiar mannerisms were meant to suggest one thing, while my actual style of wrestling absolutely suggested the opposite. When 'The Adorable one' declared that he was coming out of the closet, and that he was a homosexual - sorry mate - game over - mystery GONE!!!! They do say that imitation is the fondest form of flattery - but come on - get real - who could possibly be flattered by THAT!!!

THE TWISTED LEPRECHAUN

'Irish' Pat Barret wasn't a modest man - even though he had much to be modest about. He, like Tony Charles, my former tag-partner in 'The Welsh Wizards,' lived on Pensacola Beach. I had known Pat Barret by his real name, Ivor Barret since I first met him in Britain in 1961, when I had began wrestling for Dale Martin promotions. I never, ever liked him when I had known him in Britain, but as he was now almost a neighbor and from the old country, I tried. I really did try, but it proved impossible. Before I finally gave it up as a bad job, we had both invited each other, to each other's homes for meals etcetera. He had a really nice home on the sound side of The Gulf of Mexico. The first time I visited his home, I was mildly amazed when he introduced me to his Wife, Peggy. In all the time I had known Ivor, this was the first time I had ever seen him with a Female. I had always assumed he was queer.

Unlike Ivor, Peggy was a really nice person. The only two creatures that seemed to like Ivor, was his two Giant Rottweilers. Once again, I wondered why guys who like to appear super tough, need to surround themselves with big, ferocious Dogs.

Actually, in spite of his Dog's apparent devotion to Ivor, that very devotion almost proved fatal to him.

For whatever reason, Ivor decided to have a 'facelift'. It couldn't have impressed his Wife Peggy that much, as she left him. She said, he now looked like a big fat Chinaman. I thought he looked like a Halloween Pumpkin with the Mumps.

Ivor was at home, with only his ugly pair of Canines for company - with Ivor's new face, they must have looked like triplets. Anyway, his freshly uplifted chops, must have sprung a leak, as his face and head began to fill up with blood. In panic, he phoned his ex-wife, Peggy, and asked her to come and help him. Instead Peggy called the Hospital for help. An ambulance raced to his aid, but when they arrived at Ivor's home, they couldn't gain access, as he two giant Rottweilers got nasty and wouldn't let them in. They had to call Peggy back, and as both the Dogs knew her, she was able to go in and lock them in the garage. so that now the ambulance men could get to Ivor.

He eventually went back to live in Ireland. The last time Linda and I saw him, was at the Gulf Coast Wrestler's Reunion in 2003. Time had been cruel. Ivor used to be two or three inches taller than me, now he was much shorter. Wear and tear in the ring over the years, had really caught up with him. I had never liked Ivor, but I hate to see anyone in that condition. Multiple back surgeries had left him shrunken and semi crippled. He had been transformed from a large, tough athlete, into a little twisted Irish Leprechaun.

EMRYS

By the time Linda and I had began renting the apartment in Birmingham we also began living in the Townhouse in Gulf Breeze - we had had to wait until it became vacant, but now it was, and we were enjoying it very much. Our Master bedroom was huge. More than large enough to contain a King-sized bed and a small gym's worth of excise equipment. One entire side, was wall to wall widows, that overlooked a huge swimming pool. On two opposing walls we fitted floor to ceiling mirrors, that cosmetically made the already huge room appear absolutely enormous. The Townhouses were surrounded by a few acres of gardens. Then across the road you could access a beach that was over a couple of miles wide. If we turned right at that same road, a toll bridge would take you to Pensacola Beach. A Boardwalk with Gift Stores, Restaurants and mile upon mile of White Coral sand.

We were enjoying life - but then I received a letter from Emrys Street - that's right - my Father! He wanted to come over for a holiday. He had been to the States once before, when he stayed with my cousin, John Lewis, who lived with his Wife in New Hampshire. Apparently he had stayed with them for a few months, there was no way on Earth that I could stand that! We rushed out immediately, and I bought a plane ticket for him myself. 'Oh, how generous of you.' I hear you say. Not on your Nelly. If my Father had bought the ticket himself, he would probably end up staying with us for months - I am tough - but not that tough. The ticket I bought and sent to him, was valid for 30 days and not a second longer.

We picked him up from Pensacola airport, even on the journey back home I was becoming stressed. As I imagined, instead of thanking Linda and I for paying his airfare, he complained that it was only valid for 30 days,

"It's hardly worth coming all this way for such a short time," he moaned, "I thought I'd come over for a few months at least!"

We had hardly stepped inside our front door before he was preaching the Gospel, and treating us to his take on politics. I responded with,

"If I had had more time before your arrival, I would have put a large plaque on the wall, that read - 'The discussion of Politics, or Religion are strictly prohibited in these premises." I added, "in your own house you may be free to lecture or preach - in mine - I just don't want to know."

Talk of water off a Duck's back - it was as though he hadn't heard one word I'd said. I decided to give him my own take on his favorite subjects,

"I believe that with religion, you should believe whatever you want to believe - but don't interfere with anyone else while you're doing it. And that includes preaching about it - unless you are specifically invited to do so." He opened his gob ready to respond, but I carried right on. "In politics - vote for whoever you would prefer to screw you - and then be prepared to buy your own KY."

Did that shut him up? - DID IT HELL!!!!!

'If religious people could be reasoned with, there would be no religious people.'

Quote: Dr, House.

We didn't only have to put up with him at home, we took him everywhere with us, to the beach, where I found to my surprise, that he couldn't walk on water. We took him to all the wrestling venues where Linda and I were appearing. Mile after tedious mile, and guess what his favorite subjects were?! The former long, long journeys seemed to become longer still. Where we performed was very much part of 'The Bible Belt,' as newly converted 'good guys' Linda and I had become much more approachable. With the result, we found ourselves continually introducing my Father to our fans. Dad always made certain that they all appreciated that he was a rabid holy-roller, and got invites left right and upwards to attend their various Churches or Chapels,

"Maybe Adrian and Linda could bring you to our service this Sunday?" We heard so many times. Both they and Dad would look at me expectantly. I would adopt my most benevolent expression and reply,

"If you want my Father to come to your Church, I'll be happy to give you our address, and you can come and pick him up. Linda and I have to work every Sabbath. - Violence is Golden after all." It's strange that no one except Linda and I would be amused - HO-HUM!!!!

My Father by this time had been with us for just over a couple of weeks,

"Just about half way through our ordeal." I reminded Linda.

We were going to wrestle in Mobile that night, which was only about 70 miles from our home. Tonight I would introduce Dad to Lisa Rush and her family.

Whenever I wrestled at that arena, I would arrange for Lisa and her family to sit in a special place on the stage, near the dressing rooms. That way Lisa could accompany Linda and myself to the ring, acting as Linda's valet, and then make her way back with my gown just before the contest began. By the time my contest began, my Father, Lisa and her family would all be sitting on the stage. Behind them would be one of the TV cameras. Then also, from behind the row of chairs all the wrestlers would gather to watch the matches.

I was wrestling a huge black villain, 6foot 4inches and weighing about 280 pounds. He was a good convincing heel. After my initial dance, prance and blinding him with science, he caught me with an illegal kick. Down I went and he came down after me with a ring shaking leg-drop. Then I went through the grinder - Slam after slam, I was being devastated. I recovered - came back from the dead and left my opponent devastated, as I marched triumphantly back to the dressing room. Then it was my turn to be devastated again!!!

As I climbed onto the stage, I received such a look of anger and rage from all the other wrestlers, that one would think that I was carrying a bomb with a very short blazing fuse, or maybe the freshly severed head of Medusa.

"What's wrong with you lot?!" I demanded.

Back in the dressing room, I was enlightened.

My Father had been sitting next to Lisa during my contest. When my opponent had began turning up the heat, Lisa had winced and cried out,

"Come on Adrian, hit him back!"

My Father replied, in a thunderous voice, that he had developed in the pulpit,

"OH - IT'S ALRIGHT, LISA LOVE, HE'S ALRIGHT - WRESTLING ISN'T REAL - THEY ARE ONLY PLAYING!!!!!!!!!!!!!!!!!

CAN YOU IMAGINE THAT?!!!!!!! Right in front of the promoter, all the other wrestlers, their friends, my friends, the TV camera crew and any fans that were within range of his bloody overloud booming voice. I had never, ever discussed wrestling with my Father. I don't consider that I have had, what I would call a conversation with him in all the years I had known him, from the time I was 5 years old until now. As I say, I was devastated, embarrassed and very, very angry.

Later on our way home, I asked him why he had spouted such crap,

"Oh, that little Girl was getting upset when she thought that big wrestler was hurting you." He replied.

I made my mind up there and then, that I would never, never, ever, take my Father to a wrestling show with me again. He was with us for two more weeks. Linda and I left extra early to every venue we were to appear at - my Father was left at home. He complained bitterly, that he was bored being left at home every day. Can you imagine - he was staying in a lovely home - big swimming pool. Beautiful Gardens, just a short walk away from the beaches. If he was bored without Linda and I, then he would never know, how bored I was to be in his company.

When that day - when that 'BLESSED DAY!' came - the day he would be flying home to Wales, I could not wait to get it over with.

In those days, Pensacola Airport was very small and you could more or less arrive there mere minutes before your plane was due to leave. I told my Father, that Linda and I had to leave early for a show that night. I took him to the airport about four and a half hours before his flight and just left him there. As we raced away back to our van, I breathed a huge sigh of pure, blissful relief -

Emrys had left the building!!!

NAUGHTY BUT IT'S NICE

I'm so powerful and tough, I can never get enough,
of being mean and playing rough. But it's my only vice.
Legs to break and hair to pull, the pounding on the nearest skull.
I find quite adorable - it's naughty, but it's nice.
It's Naughty but it's nice - naughty but it's nice
let me offer you a slice - it's naughty but it's nice.
I have never understood, why I just love the sight of blood.
I can't imagine why I should, but here's some good advice.
If you play my little game, you'll be sorry that you came
and you will never be the same, it's naughty but it's nice.
If you think I'm really bad, you ought to see me when I'm mad.
I'll give you things you've never had - and you won't want them
twice.
Fists were made to punch a face, and joints to twist and then
displace,
and limbs to spread around the place. It's Naughty but it's nice.
If it should ever cross your mind, to ever try me out you'll find.
That I can be a bit unkind. You'll have to pay the price.
I really thrive on piecing moans and on agonizing groans.
I'm in love with breaking bones, it's naughty but it's nice.
There's so much I can show to you. But I must say before I do,
I need to hear a scream or two - to add a little spice.
I'll show you how to have some fun and do some things you've
never done.
I'm willing to hurt anyone - it's Naughty but it's nice.
Me without a chin to hit, teeth to break or lip to split.
Has always been a little bit like Curry without Rice.
I love to hack and bite and maul - I always have as I recall.
But these five words describe it all - it's naughty but it's nice.
It's naughty but it's nice - it's naughty but it's nice.
Let me offer you a slice - it's naughty but it's nice.

By now I had written a new album full of songs and Don
Woods was flying back over from Britain with the music to go

with them. This time he told me that we wouldn't need to go into a studio to do our recording, but we could instead record it on a reel to reel. As neither of us actually had a reel to reel, we had to go shopping for one, after Don arrived. It turned to be more difficult to locate one, than Don had anticipated. We found that our best bet was checking out all the many pawn shops that were in Pensacola. I think we must have checked them all out, by the time we finally found what we were looking for. In our last pawn shop, we were encountered by a huge, gnarled, ugly, creature, who's Hillbilly accent we both found difficult to decipher. He seemed to be having the very same problem understanding us. But eventually, he disappeared into a backroom and reappeared with an old teak reel to reel player. We were both in stitches by then, as I had noticed an enormous stuffed head of a Warthog mounted on the wall, and had suggested that it might be a self portrait of the pawn shop owner. The look he gave us, so mirrored the mounted Warthog, that I burst out laughing again. Don quickly sobered up, when he became aware of all the old rusty swords and firearms there were all around the shop. Anyway, I purchased the reel to reel, and we were in business. We spent the next couple of days recording at home. We produced the whole album on an old second hand reel to reel. Nevertheless, I still wanted to visit Dennis Stacy's WABB studio in Mobile in order to take some footage for a video from a track on my first album, that I wanted to put together. First I phoned Dennis, then I phoned Ron Goldnik to bring the TV cameras. I took costumes and makeup for Dennis, Ron, Linda and myself, then I phoned little Lisa Rush and dressed her up too, for our video. We placed Don in the control room, where he resumed his role as 'Sir Cedric'. We made a nice little video that was guaranteed air time as Ron was certain to get it played.

Soon after Ron called me, this time he had a request. There was to be a Telethon in Mobile to raise money for the Women and Children's Hospital. He invited Linda and I to help out. I suggested that it might be appropriate to invite Lisa Rush too. Well, we all spent a day answering telephones and taking pledges, and I was told later that we had helped to raise over $100,000 for the cause.

THE HUSTLER

After Linda and I had turned from hated to loved, I had wrestled against a mishmash of villains. One of them was Randy 'The Raging-Bull' Barber,' we had some excellent contests and I learned a lot from that experience. I found that I didn't have to alter my style at all. When I had danced, pranced, kissed, or patted the backsides of the Babyfaces, when I was a heel, the fans hated me for ridiculing their heroes. When I embarrassed the Bad guys by employing the exact same tactics, the fans loved it. Same for Linda, when she came to the rescue, or did something nasty to my opponent behind the referees back. They would cheer her on, then swear to the referee that she was completely innocent of the dastardly crime that the injured heel had just accused her of.

When 'Hustler' Rip Rogers arrived in the territory with his Valet Miss Brenda Briton it was like a breath of fresh air. They were great. When he first came in, after a series of wins against other Babyfaces, he began to zero in on me. He wanted to be Continental Champion.

"I came over three thousand miles to win that belt." he boomed at me from the ring after his latest victory, as I stood on the podium next to Gordon Solie. He accused me of hiding from him and such and so on. Then he threw an almighty fit when I asked him if it was he, or his Valet who was known as 'The Fleabag.' The fans were hysterical with The Hustler's furious reaction. From then on, they would chant "FLEABAG - FLEABAG - FLEABAG!!!!" every time either Rip or Brenda made an appearance. What the fans didn't know was, that Rip had made that name up himself. He suggested that I started calling Brenda that unflattering title, in order to build instant heat. That would give him a motive for any extreme tactics he would employ, in order to get even. Getting heat when wrestling with 'The Hustler' and Brenda was just like a walk in the park.

I really thought we were all made for each other. We had all kinds of contests, a Boxing match, a Texas Death match, a number of Championship matches in various venues, but if my memory serves me right, he did come 3,000 miles for nothing, and he never won my title. In one attempt, I won his valet Brenda Britton instead, and we gave her all the menial chores we could think of.

By this time there was a few more wrestlers to swell Continental's ranks. One was a guy named Jack something or other, who was doing an Arab gimmick. Much to his puzzlement, I always used to call him Mr. Off.

"Why do you always call me Mr. Off?" he asked me, "is my timing off when I wrestle, or what?"

"No," I replied, "I call you Mr. Off, 'cos your fist name is Jack."

Accompanying Mr. Jack Off, was a real blast from the past. The last time I had seen Chris Colt was when he was my tag-partner back in Britain, more than half a decade ago. He was now doing a Neo-Nazi gimmick, and was calling himself Kris Von Colt. The moment he spotted me, he once more complained that I had abandoned him in Briton and I hadn't included him, when Linda and I left there for Canada, Mexico and later the States,

"We were only tag-partners," Chris," I told him, "I didn't adopt you."

In Briton I had transported Chris back and forth to all our contests. Almost every night after the matches, we had to search for him, or wait all night for him to turn up, before our drive home. He would be as high as a kite, after he had checked out any Gay, or Leather bars in the town.

"Not any more, Chris." I told him, I decided that I would keep him very much at arm's length. Out of the ring Chris Colt was a drug addicted, alcoholic, whining drama Queen - inside the ring he was quite amazing.

Kris Von Colt was going to be Hustler Rip Rogers' tag-team partner in a contest that would reunite Rip with his valet Miss Brenda Britton, if they won the contest. On this occasion I would be partnered by Dr. Tom Pritchard. Until recently Pritchard had been a bad guy, and had been an opponent of 'Bullet' Bob Armstrong and I, when he was a part of the villainous Stud Stable.

When the contest began, both Linda and our acquisition, in the form of Miss Brenda Britton, were standing on the floor near our corner, while both Tom Prichard and I were standing on the apron, on our side of the ring. When the bell rang, I entered the ring to begin the contest. It wasn't long before the two villains began to get vicious and the rules got bent out of shape. When I thought I needed a break, I tried to tag in Tom Pritchard, but he seemed to pretend he couldn't reach my outstretched hand. The fans began to boo Dr. Tom, as he didn't seem particularly willing to help. Soon I was getting double teamed, and I really did need to tag out. Pritchard really didn't try very hard to give me a little relief, even though by now I was getting battered from all sides, by both The Hustler and Von Colt at the same time. I managed to make a comeback. It was just enough to enable me to get right into Tom Pritchard's face, in a way that he could hardly pretend that he wasn't able to reach my hand. It was then that Dr. Tom just jumped off the ring apron, and marched back to the dressing room, leaving me to fight alone. The fans screamed their disapproval at the fast fleeing traitor. What they all saw just moments earlier, was Miss Brenda Britton sneak around the ring and hand Tom Pritchard a thick wad of banknotes. I had been sold out - betrayed for cash.

Now I had a score to settle with Dr. Tom Pritchard, as well as Kris Von Colt and 'Hustler' Rip Rogers.

Rip Rogers with Brenda Briton versus Miss Linda and I had a great run. It was one of my all-time favorite feuds.

WRESTLING ROCKS

Sunday February 15th 1987.

Our very good friend Linda Marx promoted a Rock music show in the Alabama Theatre, Birmingham. It was entitled 'Shake Wrestle 'n' Roll.

THE BIRMINGHAM NEWS - By Shawn Ryan News staff writer.

Adrian Street, better known as wrestler Exotic Adrian Street, is prancing about onstage at the Moonraker nightclub.

The sky outside is drab and cloudy and wet winds are blowing. But inside Street is lighting things up on his own.

A microphone in his right hand and the chewing gum he's just plucked from his mouth in his left, Street is singing something about being as tough as Marciano and as sexy as Mae West. Twisting hips punctuate the lyrics.

Street's voice, complete with Welsh accent, borders on the off-key as he romps through the song, an autobiographical ditty named 'A Sweet Transvestite with a Broken Nose.'

Though the spectator might not know it, Street is working out, but he's not exercising his well muscled body. This workout is for his vocal cords, which need some practice before an upcoming match - a no-holds-barred, tag-team songfest, politely called "Shake, Wrestle 'n' Roll."

Yeah, you got it, a concert by singing wrestlers. Sort of a half baked glee club specializing in half-nelsons and half notes.

The concert, dreamed up by Linda Marx, publicity director for Continental Championship Wrestling, is scheduled for Sunday at The Alabama Theatre.

Among the featured performers will be Street, 'Wildcat Wendall Cooley, The Armstrongs, The Nightmares, Larry Hamilton, Gordon Solie will be MC. Local band 'Straight Talk' will provide the music. The wrestlers will provide the antics - vocal and otherwise.

"There's two purposes for the show," Ms Marx says, sitting at a ringside table in The Moonraker, "The first to put the wrestlers in a new spotlight, to show that they're not just muscle-bound idiots that can't do anything else. A lot of them have really fine educations," she says, "you wouldn't think they were as talented as they are."

She points to Street, who's kicking up his heels like a '20s flapper while he's singing about how he is as cute as Shirley Temple.

"Adrian is one of the finest artists I've ever seen," she says, "He's done some beautiful oil paintings."

Most people only see Street's in-the-ring artwork, consisting of glittering face makeup, bows in his hair and brightly colored women's clothes.

The second reason behind 'Shake Wrestle 'n' Roll' is a little less lofty. Ms. Marx says she wants to promote Continental Wrestling, which has offices in Birmingham and Pensacola. Continental holds wrestling matches each Monday night at Boutwell Auditorium. About 1,500 to 2,000 people get their weekly wrestling fix.

Wales born Street who says he's 24, but looks 10 years older [actually I was 46 at that time - but I wasn't going to tell Shawn Ryan that!] he says he expects fans to be "shocked and horrified" at Sunday's show.

Although a terror in the ring, Street in person is polite and well mannered. His ego is healthy, but he's not above making fun of himself. When someone asked him about the tightness of his pants, he replies,

"They're not pants, it's a rash."

The pants in question are a pair of Fredrick's of Hollywood Leopard-skin tights that cling to Street's lower legs like he's buttered his legs with Crazy glue.

A sleeveless, black T-shirt covers his upper half, but for a photographer's sake, it's peeled off and replaced with a trailing peek-a-boo black negligee, and with Street's barrel chest, there's a lot of boo to peek. end.

Only wrestlers would be performing. Kenny Wayne was going to do a standup comedy act, everyone else would sing. Larry Hamilton was great, he even had his own professional backup singers with him. Robert Fuller donned his big cowboy hat and accompanied himself on the guitar while he sang country and western. 'Wildcat' Wendall Cooley did a good job of 'I'm proud to be an American' and 'If heaven ain't a lot like Dixie.' I was main event and performing last - I wondered later if that had been a good idea.

I began watching the rest of the show from an upstairs window that overlooked the stage. The window was directly opposite the 'Green Room' which was liberally stocked with anything you could imagine. Linda Marx did nothing by halves.

I thought I would try a small cognac while I watched - MMMMMMMN!!! That was nice - I think I'll have another - MMMMMMMM!!!!!!! By the time it was my turn to perform, I was finding it difficult to navigate the stairs that descended down to the wings of the stage.

Next to Gordon Solie, who was making the introductions from the wings of the stage, I had placed the four costumes that I would alternately change into after each of the four songs I was going to sing. Four songs - four quick costume changes. Linda in her long Pink wig, would be banging on her tambourine, and singing backup. She was standing next to the band called 'Straight Talk.' Straight Talk was my accompanying band for the night. The first three songs and costume changes went okay for me, and the fans had really got into it. Now for my last song.

Obviously I kept 'Imagine what I could do to you' last, as my grand finale'. I quickly changed into my Glittering Gold, Purple and Lilac Gown. As the music for my song began to blare and I began strutting across the stage, I found that in my haste, I hadn't fastened my gown up properly. Then I completely forgot the words of the very song that I sang every night as I made my entrance into the ring. Just as I went dumb, my gown slid off my shoulders. DAMN!!!! I made a grab for it and I just managed to catch it before I fell over it. In a split second of inspiration, I tried to sweep the gown around in the air, as though I had meant to do that as part of my act. Instead of the graceful sweep around me that I thought would look so effective, the bloody gown wrapped around my head. Suddenly blinded, I almost stepped off the stage. I tottered precariously on the very brink of disaster. A ten foot drop into the orchestra pit would have either woke me up or knocked me out. I recovered my balance, remembered the words to end the song and got a huge reception from the fans. A reaction I didn't expect, or really deserve. Damn - it's amazing what you can get away with when the fans love you.

Mike Edison writer for 'Wrestling's Main Event Magazine writes:

'SHAKE, WRESTLE 'N' ROLL

This winter saw the passing of the Glitter King, the death of Liberace. When it came to showmanship, no one ever came close. But glitter will never go out of style, and there are those destined to pick up where Mr. Showmanship left off. Those who have always strutted with glitz and glitter and are now working harder to fill the void left by the candelabra. Exotic Adrian Street is one of those men. Both King and Queen of Continental Wrestling Promotion.

Adrian's fame stretches far beyond the confines of that promotion, however. Indeed he is an international Star, known throughout his native Europe, as he is in the Middle East, the Far East and beyond. And as of late, Adrian's reputation as the Exotic One, the most colorful man in wrestling, is stretching past the squared circle and into larger forum's of entertainment. He's been known to flirt with Hollywood, and his tasteless but tuneful LP 'Shake Wrestle 'n' Roll' has become the standard platter every time I have a cocktail party. But 'Shake Wrestle 'n' Roll' is more than just an album. It's a concept, a lifestyle, and in fact a novel and a screenplay as well. And it's all Adrian.

The Exotic One is making his ascent to Global fame [outside of his sterling rep as an ace grappler] slowly but surely, and anyone who was in Birmingham, Alabama to see Adrian's premier rock show knows that it's only a matter of time before he cracks the stigma so often cast on wrestlers and his pretty face is smeared all over People and Rolling Stone.

Marc Bolan is dead and David Bowie might as well be. Mick Jagger has proved to be the biggest disappointment of the decade and Elton John doesn't work as hard as he should. It seems that Adrian is the heir to the Glitter Throne.

The Show in Birmingham was a great success. Backed by local fave,' 'Straight Talk,' Adrian belted out a set that had the capacity audience laughing and dancing and looking forward to The Exotic One's next gig. These photos only hint at Adrian's seven costume changes and commanding stage presence, but clearly shows that 'The Bitch is Back.'

Sadly, Liberace is gone, but glitter will never go out of style, not as long as Adrian Street is around. All hail the new Glitter King! Hell - all he needs is a candelabra.

LEG-LOCK'S LIBERACE

These are the lyrics I wrote to a song that has never had any music written for.

I'm Leg-lock's Liberace, I'm Exotic Adrian Street.
I can make a Deathlock dainty - I can make a Nutcracker sweet.
I've got no Candelabra and I cannot play a note,
but I hear a Moonlight Sonata every time I grab a throat.
I'm Leg-lock's Liberace, a gaudy, glittering sight,
and I dress just like a Monarch of Destruction every night.
I'll play a Symphony on your backbone - that's sure to raise a smile.
I love a Grand Piano - but an upright is more my style.
I'm Leg-lock's Liberace and I like Leg-locks more than Liszt.
I like chopping more than Chopin - I do my Polkas with a twist.
I'll do a Rhapsody on your ribcage, or your windpipe if I choose.
So roll over and over Beethoven and give Tchaikovsky the news.

MONDAY NIGHT WARS

The WWF with nationwide TV coverage was by now already vigorously encroaching on every other regional promoter's territories. There were a few ever diminishing bastions where good wrestling could still be viewed. Then about 1988 Ted Turner, who knew even less about wrestling than Vince McMahon Jr. Bought out the WCW and wrestling went from the sublime to the ridiculous. It was bad enough that both culprits seemed determined to turn our noble sport into pure 'Showbiz,' but even in Showbiz they knew that you always left the fans wanting more, if you expected them to come back next show. Each of the two 'big' companies began competing against each other. Even if they had continued to promote 'wrestling' it would not have been good to force feed the fans they way they did, but neither company had a clue. Wrestling gave way to long, stupid, scripted, story lines, obviously written by complete idiots. Action in the ring gave way to a virtual marathon of YAP-YAP-YAP!!! There was little or no 'WRESTLING' - Wrestling had degenerated into a 'reality show' with little or no reality. In spite of that, the biggies got bigger at the expense of all the rest.

To make things worse, Ron Fuller sold Continental Championship Wrestling to David Woods owner of the TV company in Montgomery, who televised all of Continental's TV shows. David Woods then changed the name of the promotion to the CWF - Continental Wrestling Federation. Like the fore mentioned promoters, David Woods didn't have a clue what the business was about. I realized that, the moment he made Robert Fuller his booker and matchmaker. I knew then that I was about to see history repeat itself, just as I had in Britain when the Crabtree's had been given control of Televised wrestling. I groaned with despair - once more The Lunatics had taken over the asylum.

Business dropped, but was temporarily reprieved when 'Hot Stuff' Eddie Gilbert replaced Robert Fuller as Booker and matchmaker. Unlike Fuller, Eddie put the success of Continental ahead of his own agenda, even though he had ten times the wrestling ability of Fuller. Eddie made vast improvements all round. I can't remember who were his best draws, apart from Linda and I, as I was only ever interested in my own contests. He brought my old enemy in from Tennessee, 'The Superstar' Bill Dundee, not as an opponent but as my tag-team partner. It worked a treat. We had some good contests against 'Strangler' Sanders and The Russian Destroyer, also excellent contests against Lou Spicolli and Lou Fabiano. Lou Spicolli sadly died of a drug overdose just a few years later aged 27.

'Superstar' Bill Dundee and I had a good run against a number of villain teams. If I had any complaints, it would have been Dundee's over enthusiasm. In order to build up heat, it is necessary for at least one of the good guys to suffer a good thrashing and near defeat before making his heroic comeback at the end of the contest. My dilemma was, that if I allowed my opponent to hit me more than once, Bill would jump in and hit him about 28 times on my behalf. Not only did that kill the anticipation, but he was cashing in on my investment instead of me. Things changed dramatically the night 'Superstar' Bill Dundee and I went up against R.P.M. Mike Davis and Mr. Chono.

It was said that the Japanese, Mr. Chono was a very tough, no nonsense type of Wrestler. Not only had he been taught to wrestle by World Champion, Lou Thesz, but had apparently defeated the great World Champion in a 'Master versus Student contest.' If that was true, then he had to be a very good wrestler indeed. Nevertheless he proved to be a tough pro customer, especially for 'The Superstar.' I was enjoying our contest - I like wrestling, and if an opponent wants to play rough, that's fine with me. Dundee didn't seem to fare so well. Even though Bill and I were supposed to be 'The good-guys.' it was Dundee who got frustrated and brought a couple of wooden planks into the ring - one each for himself and for me. We hit Mike Davis and Chono so hard with them that they split right down the middle. Davis and Chono fled the ring, but carried on threatening Dundee from outside. I threw one of the split planks down to Chono, in order to give him an equal advantage, then I leapt out of the ring after him. We fenced furiously with the planks. I won that battle too, when I brought my plank down squarely on Chono's head. My last view of Mr. Chono was laying flat on his back in the aisle leading back to his dressing room. I was supposed to be wrestling against him the next night at a different venue. He didn't show. For some reason Mr. Chono had quit the scene.

HERE - THERE - EVERYWHERE

During this period Linda and I were in great demand by various promoters all over the States. Some we had wrestled for before, many more we hadn't.

Familiar faces were in San Antonio, Texas, still being booked by 'Sheepherders' Jonathan Boyd. Jonathan and Luke Williams. They wanted Linda and I to go back to San Antonio and wrestle for them full time, but we could not face living in hotels, or rented apartments after having a taste of living in our own property. I only agreed to fly back and forth from home in Gulf Breeze, Florida for anything up to two weeks at a time and no longer. I would wrestle in the Hemisphere in San Antonio, Austin and at 'Gilley's Club' near Houston. In San Antonio I wrestled against Big Bubba, sometimes known as 'Tugboat' Tyler. I can't remember which of those two personas he used, but I do remember him accidently stepping on my face. His great big boot split my lip, and I was disqualified for retaliating in kind. He was well over 6 feet tall and weighed 384 pounds. A guy that size definitely makes an impression - especially on your face, if he accidently steps on it.

Gilley's for me was a brand new venue, although I did wrestle a few old faces there. 'Cowboy' Scott Casey was one of my Texas favorites. On my debut in Gilley's, Scott was my opponent. That was when I made one of the most spectacular entrances of my entire career. While Scott waited impatiently in the ring, 'Imagine what I could do to you,' began playing. Then I appeared sitting on a gaudy throne, which was carried litter style by four oiled musclemen. They marched to the ring, then all around it, before I entered. I spent just enough time in the ring to decisively defeat the 'Cowboy' once again. I then left the ring in the same 'Exotic' vehicle that I had arrived in.

Talking of 'Cowboys' and 'Cowgirls.' Gilley's was full of them. The everlasting theme then began, when an announcer mentioned that he would love to watch me ride Gilley's mechanical Bull. He also wondered if I would ride it sidesaddle.

After that I never, ever appeared at Gilley's without being challenged to accept 'the challenge.' I had watched this extremely silly pastime on a few occasions. The only times I found it interesting, was when a Cowgirl with an ample bosom was in the saddle. I'm happy to say that I was never, ever stupid enough to do likewise. 'There is something very strange about a Cowboy!'

Jerry Jarrett was another promoter I wrestled for from time to time. On one such tour I teamed up with Scott Steiner. Scott and I did some very serious battering, he was a very powerful young man. On another tour, each night I wrestled one of a set of four brothers, all of whom were also 'Exotic Dancers.' Exotic Dancers with a difference. The smallest of them weighed close to 400 pounds, the largest weighed in at a hefty 560 pounds. I wrestled the biggest a few times, two of the middle-sized brothers once each. The smallest of them never turned up for our scheduled contest. The reason being that the other brothers - for a joke, had persuaded their 400 pound sibling, that I was mad at him and I intended ripping him up. I was mad at them for orchestrating such a mean ruse. Still, I suggested a way that they could earn more money as 'Exotic Dancers.'

"Begin your act completely naked," told them, "the audience would pay you a lot more to put your clothes back on!"

Wrestling for Angelo Savoldi's International World Class Championship Wrestling was a pain in the arse. We would fly up to New Jersey, where the promotion was headquartered, expecting to wrestle every single night for a week or two, only to find that half the venues had been cancelled for various reasons. It would not have been so bad if he had paid us for the cancelled shows, but for the Savoldis, no show - no pay. Eventually I had no option but to tell him to stick it, and I refused to wrestle for them anymore. But before that happened we wrestled on shows as far north as Rockland, Bangor, Lewiston, upstate New York and as far south as Virginia.

I always liked to keep my contests serious, especially when I was a heel. But when I wrestled Savoldi's Son, Joe, from the get go Linda and I would almost explode. The sole reason was Joe's choice of music, which would herald his entrance. Dire Straits' 'Money for nothing.'

After Linda and I had made our entrance to my own music - 'Imagine what I could do to you.' We would stand in our corner waiting for 'Jumping' Joe Savoldi.

The music would begin, Joe would step into the spotlight and we'd hear the lyrics 'Look at them Jo-yos' and that would set us off. By the time he entered the ring to - 'Bangin' on the bongos like a Chimpanzee' we had to hold each other up.

After we got over the giggles Joe was quite a good opponent. But throughout the contest neither Linda or I dared to look at each other. Another good opponent was Tom Brandi and also Tony Atlas, who I wrestled against in an afternoon, open-air show in upstate New York. Tony looked great. He won the posing contest - I won the wrestling match.

Bert Prentice, better known as Chris Love, and manager for Tully Blanchard and Gino Hernandez, was now promoting Universal Championship Wrestling in Wichita, Kansas. Linda and I would fly in there for him for a week or so most months. One of my first contests was against fellow Britisher Ted Heath, who now lived in Amarillo, Texas. I hadn't seen Ted since the last time we wrestled each other about a decade earlier in Britain. Ted was always one of the most awkward wrestlers I ever tangled with. He was as strong as a horse and as stiff as a short plank. I had hated wrestling with him in Britain - here in Kansas I found that nothing had changed - he was fucking awful! Still I beat him each time we met, and I went on to challenge the North American Heavyweight Champion, Rick McCord and beat him too. I was now the new North American Heavyweight Wrestling Champion.

When we wrestled in Kansas, we stayed with Bert in a beautiful house he rented that was right on a Golf Course - great for long walks. Almost all the names of the towns we wrestled in, rang a bell of the historic wild - wild West.

When we wrestled for Chris Adams' promotion in Texas, we would stay with Chris' ex-wife Jeannie Clark. Jeannie is a great character. She has recently written her own life story, which I am very sure will be very interesting indeed.

I began flying to Dallas/Fort Worth for a couple of days at a time to wrestle on a show that they televised. Mostly I flew, but if we were anywhere in the area wrestling for another promoter I would drive. On one such occasion, I drove there and arrived a few hours early. When I entered the dressing room area, I was surprised to see Kevin Von Eric already changed and ready for action. He was pacing up and down the corridor, next to a row of dressing room doors.

"Adrian - how are you man?!" He cried out as he spotted me,

"I'm doing great thanks Kevin." I replied, as he folded me in a big hug and patted my back.

"Hey man, where's Linda?" he asked.

"She'll be in, in a minute or two, I think she's getting something out of the van." I replied.

"Oh - okay - great to see you man!"

I walked to the last dressing room, which I found was empty. I stepped in, put my bag down, then looked into the dressing room next door to it. By that time Kevin was on his way back towards me,

"Adrian - how are you man?" he called, "Man you look great - Where's Linda?!"

"Thanks Kevin," I replied, "You look great too - Linda will be here in a minute." I got hugged and patted once more. As Kevin continued his marathon walk, I entered the next dressing room, finding that one empty too.

"Adrian - hey man - how are you?!" Kevin hollered as he turned and spotted me again, "Hey man - where's Linda?" This scenario was repeated every time I reappeared after checking each dressing room. I stepped out of yet another dressing room as Kevin was walking away from me, towards the entrance to the changing room area as Linda came in.

"Hey - Linda man!" Kevin hollered as he recognized her, "How are you Linda - where's Adrian?!"

We loved Kevin - he really was a nice guy - but, whatever he was on - we don't want any of it.

John Gorman, who told us he was campaign manager for the Clintons, used to run one wrestling show a month in Little Rock, Arkansas. He employed Buck Robley as his booker and matchmaker. I had met Robley before on numerous occasions. Although I don't remember if he ever wrestled on the same card as me anywhere, or if I ever saw him wrestle. Mostly he would be as high as a satellite and would want to try for even more altitude.

"Have you got any blow?" he would ask me, and after receiving my very consistent negative reply, he would always ask if I had any of a whole list of other illegal substances, that I might hopefully have about my person. Doing drugs must effect ones memory I concluded, as I have forgotten how many times I have told him that I don't do drugs of any kind. And my lapse in memory is not anything to do with drugs.

"You will never wrestle on any of my shows," Robley would then assure me, "I only use wrestlers who do drugs."

He also only used OPM - 'other people's money.' He would seduce anyone with promises of untold riches via promoting wrestling shows. Robley would then become head cook and bottle washer, and apparently he was very good at his job. His shows were consistently winners. This made him very popular with his latest investor, and all the wrestlers he employed, who he insisted were paid top dollar - of OPM. I have known many of his regular wrestlers, who will not hear a bad word spoken about Buck Robley. But considering Buck claimed he would not book a wrestler unless he was a drug addict, and that he was himself a drug pusher, you can imagine where most of the good wages earned by those wrestlers ended up. It's no wonder that Robley always insisted on paying his wrestlers top wages of OPM.

The upshot always was, that eventually, Robley would flee in the night, taking the bulk of the money due to the investor with him. Then like a poison Toadstool, he would pop up somewhere else.

"There are hundreds of suckers out there." he would declare, and he wanted a piece of all of them.

Buck Robley was really pissed off when Linda and I turned up on the show he was promoting/booking for John Gorman - especially when he found that I was to be Gorman's main event. I was really pissed off, when I found that my opponent that night would be of Buck Robley's choice.

Now I have never been accused of being a large person - especially as pro wrestlers are concerned, but Robley's choice of opponent that night would have been small for a Jockey. He was a rambunctious little twerp, who wore a mask and demanded at once that he should win our contest. I was sure that Robley put him up to making those demands. Unfortunately for the rambunctious little twerp, just meeting Robley again and finding myself in this unpleasantly unique situation, did not bode well for him - at all. I gave the arrogant little snot Nothing!!!! Nothing that is, except a fucking good hiding. I could have easily crippled him and put him out of wrestling forever if I had chosen to. I didn't want to go that far, but a Birthday party clown never bent his balloons into animals as thoroughly as I twisted that deluded little wrestling dunce. I hoped that he would be able to purchase something off Buck Robley, to help ease the pain. On one of John Gorman's shows, I would have loved to have wrestled against Buck Robley himself or his very stupid and slimy sidekick Bill Ash, but unfortunately neither of them had the guts.

I would have to say that the highlight of all of John Gorman's shows, was when he took us to the Clinton's favorite restaurant, Alouette's, when the show was over. That restaurant and the food they served was as good as anything World travelled wrestlers like Linda and I had ever encountered.

We wrestled for a new promoter in the Arkansas/Mississippi area, named John Horton. John was a nice guy, but had to be one of the biggest idiots I have ever known. To say that about somebody in my profession, that is really saying something. He was another promoter that tried to entice us away from Florida, with the idea of wrestling for him full time. In spite of my continually telling him, that I wrestled all over for many other promoters, and I most favored promoters who ran shows closer to where we lived. He persisted. When he billed me against his version of The North American Champion, I advised him to make it a non-title contest. I would never agree to lose to any of his wrestlers, and if I did wrestle his champion in a title contest - I would win. Then he would have a champion who would only wrestle for his promotion occasionally, instead of full time. Nevertheless, he insisted that he wanted me to be his promotion's champion.

"It will mean a lot more if you have it." he insisted. I couldn't argue with that, but how much would a mostly absentee champion mean to a promotion?

John's champion was his own version of 'The Spoiler.'

Don Jardine was the original 'Spoiler' and was also a very good friend of mine, so there we have another stripe against John

Horton and his ideas. The mock Spoiler was actually taller than the original and stood about 6 feet 7 inches. He really was not a very good wrestler - correction - he was not a good wrestler - yet another amendment - as far as I was concerned this guy was not a wrestler - period. Fortunately, I perfected my art in Britain, where we learned to be able to wrestle with a broomstick and make it entertaining. Even so, I had my work cut out.

Against my better judgment, I beat his 'Spoiler' winning the championship belt. Then told him that his new champion would be a fairly infrequent contestant on any of his future wrestling shows. Every time I did make the trip, I told him that he needed to put the championship belt around one of his regular wrestlers waists. The monumental problem with that scenario was, that he didn't have a single wrestler who was good enough to take it from me. The last time I wrestled for John Horton, he shocked me once again. I really didn't think he could ever come up with any ideas more ridiculous than the ones he had ran by me in the past. I had no sooner stepped into the dressing room and dropped my wrestling bag, when John handed me a stack of about ten paper pages.

"What's this?" I asked him.

"That's your contest," he told me, the idiot had written a move for move script.

"WHAT?!!!!" I roared.

"Read it." he insisted, "It's really good - I want to know what you think of it."

"I can tell you what I think of it without wasting my time reading it." I told him. "First of all, eat a whole boiled cabbage, a couple of pounds of prunes, then wash it all down with a quart of olive oil. then this crap paper might be useful to you!"

This same guy used to order wrestling outfits from us for his wrestlers. That was good. What wasn't good was, that he insisted on designing the outfits himself, when he didn't have a clue how to do it. I told him again and again, if we made the outfits the way he designed them, rather than the correct way, they would not only be substandard, but they would be three times more expensive to make.

"That's okay," he would respond, "the wrestlers will be paying for them themselves." He never, ever stopped trying to convince me that he actually knew something about wrestling or designing wrestling wear. I snatched his ten page script back out of his hands when he once again tried to insist I read it. I tore it into tiny shreds,

"Cancel the prunes." I told him, as I showered him with confetti. Then I told him the way things were going to go that night.

Many of his wrestlers - well I'll call them wrestlers for want of a better word - many of his wrestlers were substandard copies of more famous originals. One of these was a real life-sized copy of 'The Undertaker'. This Undertaker had the complete costume that was worn by the original at that time. What he didn't have was one tenth of the original's wrestling prowess and charisma. Nevertheless I saw a major role for this doppelganger and a way out of remaining John Horton's Champion.

This is what happened.

My opponent made his entrance, then Linda and I made ours. Preliminary's over, I began to beat the living crap out of my opponent for about ten painful minutes. As Linda was ringside, leaning forward on the ring apron, watching the massacre. Then, the phony Undertaker crept up behind her. He suddenly made a grab and picked her up onto his shoulder and began to walk away with her. At first I appeared to be unaware of her predicament, as I tried to find an area on the body of the phony 'Spoiler' that I hadn't kicked or punched yet. By the time I was made aware of Linda's ringside abduction, my in ring opponent was completely out of it. Then I dove out of the ring, chased after the fake Undertaker, and began to do to him, what I had just left off doing to my opponent. Meanwhile the referee had began to count. My opponent, with the help of the ropes managed to haul himself to his feet before the count ended, meanwhile I was still outside the ring treating the Undertaker in a manner that could easily make him a customer for another undertaker. And that Ladies and Gentlemen was how I was able to give the phony Spoiler his title back.

I would wrestle for Jody Hamilton in Georgia anywhere from a few days to a couple of weeks at a time. I had first met Jody in Crockett's promotions when he and his partner wrestled as 'The Assassins.' Jimmy Valiant and I had been embroiled in a feud against them when they had been managed by Paul Jones. Later when we first lived in Gulf Breeze, Florida, Jody had been a neighbor who lived less than 100 yards away from us. He wrestled there as 'The Masked Flame'. We often traveled back and forth to the venues where we wrestled each night.

Now in Georgia, Jody ran a wrestling school and also promoted his own wresting shows.

We wrestled for Global Championship Wrestling in lower Florida for about one week out of every month. Bob Roop, former Olympic Greco-Roman Wrestler was the booker. They did have some great wrestlers there at that time including Professor Malenko's two sons, Joe and Dean. The first time we visited their office, I saw a face I had not seen for decades Standing outside the entrance to the gym.

"Do you know Karl Gotch?" Bob Roop asked me.

"Last time I saw Karl was back in Britain, about a quarter of a century ago." I replied.

"Karl doesn't like your gimmick!" Roop told me, in a voice loud enough for Karl Gotch to hear.

"I don't much like his gimmick either!" I answered, in a voice that matched his in volume. Karl Gotch just smiled and walked back into the gym.

Another face I hadn't seen since before we left Britain, was that of Jackie Pallo Jr. When I did see that face it was in the opposite corner of the ring from where Linda and I stood. We had a good 'British style' contest, which I ended with my pinning him for the victory with a 'special leg-grapevine' and my own version of a wrestler's bridge.

Linda often wrestled for Global too, her best contests were against 'Grizzly' Smith's Daughter, 'Rockin' Robin and the snarling, screaming Luna Vachon.

We always flew to lower Florida when we wrestled for Global, so we needed to be transported from our hotel to the various venues. We were picked up each evening by Ward Hall and C.M. Christ, who also scouted for Global's future venues. Both Ward and C.M. became great friends of ours. They were Circus and Carnival folk, and they exhibited freaks and oddities all over the States. I still have a book written by Ward entitled

'My very UNUSUAL Friends.' which pictures - well - all his very unusual friends.

My all time highlight of the times we wrestled for Global, was at a very large club. I was in the dressing room preparing for my contest, when a security guard walked in and said,

'Nature-Boy' Buddy Rogers is outside, and asked if he could come into your dressing room to meet you?" The look I gave the security guard would have done credit to Medusa. Obviously this was a joke that one of the other wrestlers hoped to pull on me. So I casually replied,

"Yes of course 'Nature-Boy' Buddy Rogers can come in to meet me - But while you're at it, will you tell the Pope and Queen Elizabeth, that they will have to go to the back of the queue?!"

My jaw dropped onto my chest as 'Nature-Boy' Buddy Rogers walked into my dressing room and shook my hand.

"I was sunbathing on the beach, when an airplane flew over pulling a banner with your name on it, advertizing the wrestling he told me."

I was as excited while I was in the ring wrestling that night, knowing that one of my all time heroes was watching me perform, as I would have been, if it had been me watching 'Nature-Boy' Buddy Rogers wrestling when he was in his prime. WOW WHAT A BLAST!!!!!!!

I wrestled for Randal Brown in Georgia, he really was a great guy, we had a lot of fun together. Whenever we meet up with him again, for any of the wrestler's reunions we may attend, he always reminds me of the day we were traveling together to one of his venues. On the way, we stopped for some refreshments. After we got seated, we were approached by the waitress. She was really giving me the strangest looks, as though she couldn't believe her eyes. So when I made my order, I asked,

"Do you serve homosexuals my dear?"

she answered, "Er-a-um er Yeah, I guess so."

"OH, how lovely,' I replied, "then I would like to order two." Randal began laughing and from that day he has never ever stopped.

After Randal heard of the success that Linda Marx had had when she promoted 'The Shake Wrestle 'n' Roll Concert' in Birmingham, Alabama, he wanted to promote it too. The only difference was, that I would be the only singer, and the rest of the show would be wrestlers, wrestling. The first was such a success and he promoted a couple more. Then I got a call from Bert Prentiss [Chris Love] he was now living in North Carolina, and he wanted to promote a Wrestling Fan-fest, which would include me singing my own songs. That turned out to be a show I would always remember. The reason that this show was so special to me, wasn't so much my performance, but who I would be performing for. It turned out to be a real 'Star-studded' audience. Tully Blanchard and his Dad Joe was there. Joe Pedicino and World Champions Lou Thesz and one of the greatest of all time - 'Nature-Boy' Buddy Rogers. When I completed my act, we all mingled and I really enjoyed all the compliments I received from some of the best ever to share my profession. Bill Apter was there, to cover the event for the Pro Wrestling Illustrated magazine that he wrote for. I was thrilled that as Lou Thesz, Buddy Rogers and myself had all been World Champions, Apter wanted a photo of the three us standing together. Bill Apter promised that he would send me a copy of that photo as soon as he had one in his hand. That must have been at least a couple of decades ago - I'm still waiting. Until he keeps his promise, you will never, ever, hear me say a good word about Bill Apter.

We often worked in the East coast of Florida for various promoters, or the St Petersburg/Tampa area for Kevin Sullivan, who was booking for that promotion. We rarely stayed at a hotel on those trips, but usually stayed with either Kevin and Nancy or with Dory Funk Jr. and his Wife Marty.

When I wrestled in the St Petersburg/Tampa area a frequent opponent turned out to be Barry Horowitz. I had wrestled with him many time before for Crockett's promotion when he had wrestled as Jack Hart. I had been a villain in all of those previous contests and Jack Hart had been the Baby-Face. I didn't like Jack Hart personally, I found him extremely irritating. My opinion of him translated into some rough treatment for him whenever we shared the same ring. BUT - Barry Horowitz who now wrestled villain to my Baby-Face, was a breath of fresh air, and a really good, proficient opponent. I looked forward to every action packed contest I had with him. His transformation was really most remarkable.

For other promotions on Florida's East coast I wrestled occasionally during this period. One contest was against 'The Honky-Tonk-Man' Wayne Farris. In all the years we had both been wrestling, this was the very first time we had ever met each other.

"How are you Adrian - what are you going to do to beat me tonight?" he asked me in the way of greeting.

I do appreciate an opponent that submits to the inevitable.

I wrestled in a large semi open air pavilion that was set up in a huge Fairground. The wrestling was free to anyone who bought a ticket to the fair. Not knowing how far this venue was from home, Linda and I gave ourselves plenty of time and arrived in the afternoon for an evening show. We were both surprised to see Dory Funk Jr. standing in the ring. He was already changed into his wrestling gear and ready for action. As we chatted to Dory, a few people wandered in from the fair and sat down. I then took my wrestling bag to the dressing room. By the time Linda and I returned to ringside, there were probably a couple of dozen or so men, women and kids sitting around the ring, just looking at Dory who was just standing in the corner of the ring.

"Let's have a pull around, Adrian." Dory invited. Both Linda and I laughed - we obviously thought he was joking. He wasn't. I really don't even like to be seen by the fans before I actually make my entrance into the ring, but I liked Dory and decided to humor him. I hadn't changed and was just wearing the same clothes I had been traveling in, but I climbed into the ring, shook hands and began to wrestle. Damn, we were there grappling for the rest of the afternoon. By the time we shook hands and left the ring, there were more fans watching, but no more than a hundred. The wrestling show proper, was not due to begin for at least a couple more hours, and I've wondered ever since that day why, Dory was compelled to give a few fans a freebie. But he was acting very strange that day. After the show began, and he had wrestled his own contest, he got right into Dan 'The Beast' Severn's face and they ended up having a shoot as an extra unscheduled contest.

I was wrestling against 'Thunderkat' in a challenge match that pitted my golden locks against his Mask. I won the contest and the Mask. Before Linda and I left for home, I gave Thunderkat his Mask back. The poor bugger didn't have another one with him which he needed to wear when he wrestled again the next night. - See what a nice guy I am?!!!

PEACH STATE WRESTLING

Ben Masters promoted Peach State Wrestling in Americus and Cordele in Georgia. Ben was a great guy and an excellent promoter - every show I wrestled for him was always packed to capacity.

I am not really a big fan of Battle Royals, I much prefer just one opponent - to me that makes it an equal contest. But, there were two Battle Royal contests that I wrestled in for Ben. One featured both Men and Women wrestlers. The contestants included Bambi, Peggy Lee Leather, Ronnie Garvin and Jake 'The Snake' Roberts'. The other one was 'WHO CAN STOP THE BUTCHER BATTLE ROYAL'. That contest featured a ring full of wrestlers including Rob Van Damme, Mick Foley, Tony Atlas, Buff Bagwell and of course 'The Madman from the Sudan' Abdullah the Butcher. Abdullah appealed more to the very bloodthirsty amongst wrestling fans. Whenever The Butcher appeared there was a guaranteed BLOODBATH. I believe there is a place for bloody contests in the wrestling business, but they should only take place rarely, and for a specific reason. I found that the more often the fans saw blood, the less it meant. Obviously, it wasn't at all unusual to bleed during a contest, some wrestlers punch and kick very hard, some are very clumsy. But Abdullah The Butcher carried a razor blade taped to a stick and he was very generous when it came to wielding it. He would not only slash the hell out of any opponent he was pitted against, but would always slash the hell out of himself too. His head carried more lines than Clapham-Junction Railway Station. As I say, that's okay if you like that sort of thing, but it's not for me. I had told him in previous contests, but to be sure, I warned him again. I told him that, if he so much as came within razorblade's range of me during the entire contest, I would kick him so hard, that his testicles would end up where his eyeballs used to be. He never, ever came close. The only time that Abdullah and I might touch during one of these contests, would be when I helped a few other wrestlers heave the Butcher's 360 pound bulk over the top rope in order to eliminate him from the contest.

I did wrestle in single contests against most of the wrestlers who were featured in the Battle Royals and never lost one of them. I also wrestled against the 400 pound, Ronnie P Gossett in a one on one contest. The loser of the contest would have to wear a Ladies dress. From what I'd heard of Ronnie, he would have fought a lot harder if it was the winner who would be made to wear the dress. Well Ronnie lost and so was entitled to wear the dress, but he was so grossly fat, that he looked like a walking, talking Waterbed. Hardly a figure for the Catwalk at a fashion show.

I had quite a feud going against Steve 'The Brawler' Lawler. He was over 6 feet tall and weighed 256 pounds. He was rough, tough, and energetic - just the way I like 'em. We knocked lumps off each other. The climax of our feud was a 'Baby Bottle/Baby Bonnet' Contest. The loser to wear a Baby Bonnet and suck on a Baby's bottle. Well we sure as Hell didn't fight like infants - BUT - after the dust settled and all was said and done - Steve 'The Brawler' Lawler made a really cute Baby-Boy.

WOW was a Japanese funded promotion ran by Rip Tyler. All their shows were taped for Japanese TV in a studio in Pensacola. The fact that it was in Pensacola, and just a very short drive from home, for me was its greatest appeal. My best opponents were Marcel Pringle and Bob Holly - both of which I beat soundly. Unfortunately, the promotion didn't last.

BLIND AS A BAT

Mike Danger was as blind as a Bat. According to him, he had been a super dare Devil Skateboard Champion, who, while attempting to break some speed record collided with an eighteen wheeler. According to Mike, that was how he lost his sight. I heard that the real reason he became legally blind, was that he didn't like taking the diabetes medicine he had been prescribed. But he did come up with a catchy image. He wore a complete Batman suit into the ring and wrestled as 'Blind as a Bat' Mike Danger. As he really was blind, his 'Batmask' didn't have eyeholes, which proved that Mike was the genuine article. I first met Michael Aperton, Mike's real name, when he came to Skullkrushers and asked me to train him as a pro wrestler. Mike was one of the most un-trainable pro wrestling wannabes I had met. But, he had a friend who owned a fair size bar called T-Bears and Mike began promoting wrestling shows there every Tuesday Night. What was even better was, that T-Bears was only about 60 miles or so from home. Linda and I were paid top dollar and our services were required every Tuesday night. Many of my Skullkrusher wrestling students got to make their debut there.

Unfortunately, at his own insistence, so did Mike Danger. Obviously with such a severe disability our blind 'Superman' couldn't appear as a villain, so we had to create a suitable nemesis for him. Enter Theodore E McErvin. He was better known as 'Turbo Ted'. Even though he was already wrestling, he was a regular at Skullkrushers. He had been taught initially by Norman Charles, who was originally from Britain's Wigan area. I first met Norman when he wrestled in Britain as Maurice La Rue. Norman Charles had ran a wrestling school for a number of years. He very much believed in teaching the craft of wrestling 'The Hard Way.' First you would pay your fee - then you would be introduced to just how painful Pro wrestling can be. If you couldn't absorb the agony - PISS OFF! That was his school's motto. Many of my students were frightened to death of Ted, and with good reason -

Ted was rough - VERY ROUGH! Ted had been taught the hard way - he really didn't know any other way.

It was obvious that a very nasty villain would be far too much for a blind competitor to handle. But, I thought of a great angle to use as an equalizer. In order to make it into a more equal contest, Mike's opponents should be blindfolded. Then if anything, the advantage should go to Mike Danger, as he was used to not being able to see. Also it gave the villain a huge advantage for drawing heat, by simply craftily lifting the blindfold whenever he thought the referee might be distracted. As I had imagined their contest did get great heat, but poor Mike had a nasty habit of getting exhausted within minutes of entering the ring, and then throwing up his lunch. Match over, he would then rush back to the dressing room and scream the roof off that Turbo Ted had kicked him too hard in the stomach. I am the one who should have complained - I often had to wrestle in the same ring after Mike Danger - that could be messy.

I wrestled a lot with Turbo Ted myself - yes, he could be a mean handful. I would beat on him until I was in pain, chase him back to the dressing room, then when I returned to the ring, I would challenge him to come back and finish our disagreement for good. I would have already told him before our contest began - NOT TO COME BACK TO THE RING - UNDER ANY CIRCUMSTANCES!!!!! I would call him back into the ring - the fans would call him back into the ring, AND DAMN WITHOUT FAIL - HE WOULD COME RUNNING BACK INTO THE RING. I would then be forced to start all over again, beating the crap out of him - then chasing him back to the dressing room. So yet again I would challenge him to return and finish our fight and the SILLY BASTARD WOULD COME!!!!!! Ted was not supposed to come back to the ring at all, after I had first chased him out of it. I would brand him as a coward - the crowd would really want to see him get his comeuppance, but that was what was going to bring them back next week. Ted was giving them next week for free. I tried and tried to explain the psychology, but Turbo Ted lived on an entirely different Planet.

For whatever reason Mike was obsessed with Missy Hyatt, it was obvious why some men were attracted to her - but, Mike was blind. Anyway, he brought her in as an opponent for Linda. Linda turned her upside-down, inside out and outside in! Mike had already booked her to come back for a return contest - I was not surprised that she didn't show. One of my favorite opponents at T-Bears was Marcelle Pringle, we had some wars. In tag-team contests, my partner was usually a young black wrestler, who had 'borrowed' the name of one of the old time greats - Bobo Brazil.

Dodi was a good friend as well as a good promoter, we worked on most of her shows. She was always willing to give very many of my Skullkrusher's wrestlers their first contests. Her favorites from my school became regulars at her venues, many of whom, I wrestled myself. Two of my favorites were Dave Lewis, who first wrestled as the villainous 'Knight Templar'. He later changed his image to a Babyface, 'The American Warrior'. As his name suggests, he adopted a patriotic version of the 'Ultimate-Warrior'. The main difference was that Dave Lewis' Warrior was a much better wrestler than the 'Ultimate' version. My other favorite was Brian Strickland. With my permission he wrestled as 'Skullkrusher' Brian Strickland. Brian idolized me, he even named his new Baby Son Adrian. After he first began to wrestle at Skullkrushers, he grew his naturally blond hair long like mine. A few years later when I shaved my head, Brian shaved his too. I even designed his ring-wear, like the studded leather costumes that I had worn myself. I must have wrestled against Brian for almost every promoter that I wrestled for during this period. He also had great contests against Jake 'The Snake' Roberts, Greg 'The Hammer' Valentine and 'Road Dogg' Jesse James. Unfortunately Brian died in the ring during a contest in August 2011. He was still a very young man, but he had allowed himself to balloon up to about 300 pounds. Another case of digging his own grave with a spoon. The last Skullkrusher student I wrestled for Dodi was Drew 'Blood' Bennet. Unfortunately, now Dodi is no longer with us either.

I wrestled Gemini for Dodi and Continental. I also had a short feud with another Skullkrusher 'Filthy' McNasty.

I wrestled a couple of times in Philadelphia. The first time was against my old opponent, then later, tag-team partner, Boogey-Woogie-Man, Jimmy Valiant. Jimmy had been frightened out of his wits when we had first met for Jimmy

Crockett's promotion. He admitted then, that he knew nothing about wrestling, and he was not exaggerating.

"I'm not a wrestler," he told me, "I don't know how to get into those holds - I don't know how to get out of them. If you get me in any of your wrasslin' holds Brother, I'll be there till you let me loose!"

As my tag-partner, Jimmy had had a ringside seat every night, and saw firsthand what I was capable of. Now the poor bugger was once again my opponent, and he was not a happy camper. I tried my very best to make some of his offence look convincing, but his heart was not in it. Eventually I just had to bury him. I got Linda to hit him on the back of his head with her loaded golden Boxing glove, in order to give him an excuse for loosing, but the Boogie-Woogie-Man really didn't have a clue. He had flamboyance in spades, but that was it.

I have found that most flamboyant wrestlers, myself included, used their flamboyance to disguise a flaw. My flamboyance helped to initially distract attention from my smaller stature. The feathered ponytails, made me look taller. My bizarre dress and mannerisms, would also detract from my size. Then after disrobing and coming to grips with my very much larger opponent, it was then my superior wrestling skill that grabbed the attention.

What many other wrestlers used flamboyance for, was to help disguise the fact that they couldn't actually WRESTLE to save their lives.

What helped them more, was that a colorful character like Jimmy Valiant did put arses on seats. That would also make him very popular with the promoter. The promoter would make sure that a crowd puller was a winner. If the promoter matched a crowd puller with a good straight, credible wrestler, and ordered that the crowd puller win, then the REAL wrestler's credibility would rub off, and make the fans think that someone like Jimmy Valiant was a World-beater.

The other Philadelphia contest was a tag-team contest that pitted 'The Spoiler' Don Jardine and myself versus Kevin Von Eric & Freebird 'Michael Hayes.'

Don warned me before we entered the ring to be very careful of both opponents,

"Kevin can be really accidently clumsy, and Hayes will hurt you on purpose - if you let him." He told me.

I had already heard about one of Kevin Von Eric's accidents. After slamming an opponent to the mat, Kevin climbed onto the corner post in order to perform his signature finish. He dove up into the air with the grace and buoyancy of an Angel, but landed like a ton of bricks with his knee right into his opponents chops. But, of course, that wasn't Kevin's fault. He blamed someone in the back of the arena, who must have turned the volume of the air conditioner up just as Kevin took his big dive.

"The extra volume of air blew me off course." he claimed.

There was no accidents that night from Kevin, but when I first came to grips with Michael Hayes, I could see that Don had really assessed him correctly. He was stiff - I actually got a flashback to the first time I wrestled against Keith 'Blood-Boots' Martinelli in his hometown of Bolton years ago. That had been a lesson in 'if your opponent hits you too hard - hit him back harder!' Keith became one of my favorites and a great friend. I adopted the same tactics with Michael - I'm happy to say that we have been great friends since that night.

I had a series of contests against Ed Farhat, the 'original' Detroit Sheik in Cleveland and Warren Ohio. If this guy wasn't completely nuts, he was one hell of a great actor. The first time I set eyes on him, Linda and I were already in the ring, impatiently awaiting his arrival. Eventually he began his entrance which seemed to take forever. We wondered who must have been brave enough to open this madman's cage. He approached the ring one slow step at a time. He crouched and stared wide eyed all around him. He looked terrified, as though all the Ogres and Demons of Hell were swirling around his head. In the time it took him to actually enter the ring, I could have strolled back to the dressing room and performed another ten sets of pushups. Then, even when he did finally enter the ring, his strange performance still continued. Dropping onto his knees, he began chanting and praying to some other mystical being. Damn if this guy didn't already have enough problems, he now had me to contend with.

The bell rang and the Sheik exploded out of his corner like a shot from a cannon. I saw that he was already armed with a weapon that I had been previously warned against. In his right fist I saw that he was carrying his famous loaded pencil. A stick that was attached to a razor sharp blade. With this very same instrument the Sheik had carved bloody scars into so many of his famous opponents for so many years. Abdula the Butcher, Bobo Brazil, Terry and Dory Funk Jr. Bruno Sammartino, Dick the Bruiser, Freddie Blassie, John Tolos and many more.

Now it was my turn to bleed. NOT TONIGHT JOSEPHINE - I DON'T PLAY THAT GAME!!!!!!! As the Sheik charged me and screamed his war cry, wielding his savagely loaded pencil, I threw up my forearm and knocked it right out of his grasp. I then quickly gathered it up and stabbed the Sheik in the head repeatedly with his own blade. He wanted blood - now he had it - he was covered - I was covered and so was the ring, and not one drop of it was mine. The whole contest only lasted a very few minutes after the bell had sounded. It had taken 'The Wildman from Syria' ten times longer than that to get from his dressing room to the ring. I had a few more contests against the Sheik, each one a very close repetition of the first.

The last time I wrestled Ed Farhat was almost a mirror image of all the others. But, this time when he charged me, I grabbed him and used his own impetus to spin him around, slamming him violently into my corner post. I snatched his sharpened pencil out of his grasp and once more began stabbing him in the head. It was then that I felt a tremendous blow from behind, which all but knocked the wind out of me. It was The Detroit Sheik's reinforcements. The 'Iron Sheik' had crept into the ring and had delivered a powerful kick right into the small of my back. I bit the canvas, then rolled sideways to avoid being stomped on by one of the Iron Sheik's big curved toed boot. I rolled again and was narrowly missed by a mighty stomp from Ed Farhat's big curved toed boot. I rolled onto my hands and knees and flew right between the Iron Sheik's legs, then in the same direction right between the legs of Sheik Ed Farhat. They both began leaping around the ring attempting to stomp me, while I continued to dive between their legs to avoid being flattened by their big curly Aladdin style booties. It must have looked like the crazy Dance of the Camel Jockeys. The fans were screaming at the top of their lungs. At last I dived between a pair of legs, out of the ring and raced back to the dressing room as fast as my very swift legs would carry me. I returned to the ring with reinforcements of my own. The 6 foot 8 inch, 290 pound, Big Bruiser Brody. Bruiser and I exploded back into the ring and battered the two Sheiks silly. After the Bruiser and I had bruised our fists and feet severely, The Sheiks bailed out of the ring. I grabbed the microphone from the timekeeper and challenged the Sheiks to meet Big Bruiser Brody and me in a tag-team contest on the very next show in that arena. They accepted our challenge, the contest was due to take place on the 3rd of August.

Unfortunately Bruiser Brody took a tour of Puerto Rico before our contest took place. In a dispute between himself and Puerto Rican Wrestler Jose Huertas Gonzales, Big Bruiser Brody was stabbed to death in the shower room. The date of Bruiser's death was on July 17th 1988. That was just two weeks shy of our scheduled contest against The two Villainous Sheiks.

BEAUTY - THE BEAST & DOWNTOWN BRUNO

I don't need to search for someone to adore, I've already given up
my heart.
And the love I have is all accounted for, I've fallen for a gorgeous
work of art.
When I want to see the fairest of them all, and gaze into those
sexy eyes of blue.
I walk up to my full length mirror on the wall,
I take a breath and just admire the view.
Cos' I'm in love with me, so in love with me.
It isn't hard to see, why I'm so in love with me.
When I comb my hair in the looking glass, I find, I have a job to
drag myself away.
I find it very difficult to get me off my mind,
but that's the price perfection has to pay.
I'm in love with me, so in love with me.
It isn't hard to see, why I'm so in love with me.
I love my perfect body and my flashing film star grin.
I fall in love with everything I see.
And though I try to fight it, I don't think I'll never win.
I really get a big kick out of me.

I received a phone call from 'Superstar' Bill Dundee. He told
me that he had created an opponent for himself with a similar
persona to my own. He then asked my permission to allow them
to use my song, 'I'm in love with me.' for their videos etc.

"His real name was Terry Simms, but wrestled as Terry 'The
Beauty' Garvin," Dundee explained, "he has a huge bodyguard
named Marc Gullen they called 'The Beast' and their manager
was 'Downtown' Bruno."

Garvin who claimed to be from 'The City of Pretty,' used to
wear a Pink sweat suit - like I used to when I had first wrestled in
Tennessee. He also used to insist that his own Pink mat be spread
over the ring canvas before he would enter the ring each night.

"I don't was my body where other wrestlers have had their sweaty bodies." he would remark. I always thought that that was a very clever touch.

Garvin and company had then began attacking Dundee verbally and physically any and every time the opportunity arose. Things had become so dangerous for 'The Superstar' that he could not even find himself a tag-partner to fight with him against the formidable duo of Terry 'The Beauty' Garvin and Marc 'The Beast' Gullen. After the videos were made for 'Beauty and the Beast' using my song 'I'm in love with me,' Garvin claimed that the song was written and performed by himself.

In order to defend himself, Bill Dundee claimed that he was going to bring in 'A mystery tag-team partner' to help him to take care of Beauty, the Beast and Downtown Bruno. During a TV interview, while he explained to commentators Lance Russell and Dave Brown, what he intended doing, he was rudely interrupted by Beauty and company.

"You haven't got a mystery partner," Garvin screeched, "nobody wants to tag with you - you're finished, everyone is scared of us!"

"Okay," reasoned Dundee, "if you don't believe I have a tag-partner, just turn around, he's right behind you!"

'I'm not falling for that old trick!" Garvin declared. It was then that I belted both the Beauty and the Beast from behind and after a little scuffle they quickly departed.

In order to show the television audience our combined tag-team skills, Bill and I then took part in a contest against 'The Hollywood Blonds.' Then while we were thus engaged, we were suddenly outnumbered, when Garvin and all his cronies hit the ring and with the help of the Blonds attacked Dundee, Linda and myself viciously.

The scene was set for a big grudge match at the Mid South Coliseum the following Monday, and the beginning of one hell of a blood feud that would last for months to come.

I was still wrestling close to home, but would drive back and forth to the bigger shows in Tennessee for these arena filling contests.

The presence of Linda and I completely turned the tables on the terrible trio. We beat them in contest after contest. In order to punish Downtown Bruno for his perpetual interference, we challenged them to a contest that pitted The Beauty, The Beast and Downtown Bruno against 'Superstar' Bill Dundee, Miss Linda and myself. There was an added stipulation, and that was, that whoever lost the deciding fall, would get their heads shaved bald in the ring.

The bad guys enjoyed speculating which one of us would be the most upset sporting a big bald head. They could never really make their minds up who they would enjoy humiliating the most. Garvin thought that it would most probably be Miss Linda who would soon resemble a brand new Q-ball. They obviously did not know what Miss Linda was capable of. The action was outrageous, we all knocked lumps off each other. But, when Downtown Bruno and Miss Linda locked horns, both Beauty and the Beast cheered with glee, as they imagined that this would soon end the contest in their favor. They couldn't have been more deluded. Linda tore Bruno to shreds, she hoisted him into the air and slammed him down so hard that the ring shook. After Linda took the winning fall, it was Bruno who sat in the Barber's chair. Mind you, I thought the Q-ball look suited him.

Once more we were challenged to a 'looser gets his head shaved contest' between Beauty and the Beast against 'Superstar' and me. The Beast got shaved. I challenged The Beauty Garvin to a one on one looser gets his head shaved - he declined.

That ended our Beauty and the Beast feud in Tennessee - but the story was not over yet.

BEAUTY - THE BEAST & THE VAMPIRE BARONESS

Terry 'The Beauty' Garvin along with his Beast suddenly arrived in Continental, and immediately began bragging during his first TV interview with Charlie Platt that he had written and performed my song 'I'm in love with me'. Not only did he have his music videos shown during his interview, but in order to add credence to his claim, he showed my vinyl album onto which he had pasted his own photograph. That was when Linda and I hit the scene and confronted them.

"Everyone knows that 'I'm in love with me' is my music - everyone knows that I wrote it and it's me singing!" He told me and everyone at home watching their TVs. In order to add validity to his claim, he held up 'MY' record album on which he had affixed his own photo.

"See - my photo - on my album!!! He claimed again. Then Linda got right into his face.

"You are a liar!" she told him, "I saw you sticking your own silly photo on Adrian's record album!" With that Linda snatched the album out of Garvin's grasp and tore his photo off, revealing my album with my photos on it.

"You shut your mouth - you floozy!" Garvin screamed back at Linda.

"WHAT!!!" Linda screamed back at him and walloped him in his chops in emphasis. Their attempt at retaliation brought me into the fray, which caused the enemy to retreat back to the sanctuary of their dressing room.

I wasted no time issuing our challenge, against what I now called Terry 'The Booby' Garbage. I was surprised that he accepted my challenge, considering what I had done to him and his associates when I wrestled them in Memphis. But, as I should have suspected,' Booby and the Beep' had a plan. I outwrestled, out-dazzled and outsmarted Garvin. But I was suddenly outnumbered, just as I was about to score the winning fall. 'The Beast' dove into the ring and whacked me on the head with a huge bone that he always carried into the ring. His attack on me, brought Linda into the ring, and into harm's way. Garvin grabbed her and slammed her to the mat. He then held her down, while The Beast hammered the bone down repeatedly onto Linda's left arm. I tried to defend her, but got clobbered from all sides. Both Linda and I were now receiving the beating that Garvin had promised us. Then help arrived from an unexpected source. A figure hurled himself into the ring and began throwing dropkicks, fists and forearm smashes at my two enemies. I managed to rally enough, to clear the two violent villains out of the ring.

"WE'LL BE BACK - WE HAVEN'T FINISHED WITH YOU YET STREET!!!" Garvin screamed. Now it was I who needed a tag partner.

I chose the young blond-haired wrestler named Todd Morton, who had just rushed to our aid, as my new tag-partner. It was reported that Linda's left arm had been broken. But as there was now Todd Morton, Miss Linda and I against the villains, the odds were not right. Three against two is okay, if it's in the heel's favor, but not the other way round. To play a credible hero, you have to fight uphill battles.

So, in order to make a better balance, I phoned a Lady that we had known since our early days in Continental. Her name was Diane O'Farrell. Diane used to write a column for a newspaper in Panama City. She was obviously drawn to the unusual, as very many of her best stories were of Linda and I. Diane was obviously a big fan of the Bizarre, as her garb and appearance became more and more Gothic-like every time we saw her. Her skin was naturally as white as a ghost - her hair as white as snow. Even without her jet black make up, she was strange. So were all her friends that she introduced us to. One guy with a shaven head and a body covered with tattoos, was skewered with enough metal to make a military tank. He also kept a live pet Leopard in the back of his car. Eventually Diane became known as 'The Baroness.' She had Vampire like fangs permanently bonded to her own canine teeth. Then she began driving a Hearse, complete with a coffin in the back. The first time I saw her drive up in it, I remarked, tongue in cheek,

"Come on Diane, anyone can drive a regular black hearse - but I would be much more impressed if it was a bright, hot pink."

I was joking, but next time we saw Diane her hearse was the hottest pink you can imagine. "Now that's class!" I told her - tongue in cheek .

She immediately agreed to join up with Beauty and The Beast, as their valet, and became the bad guy's new weapon to counterbalance our Miss Linda.

We would wrestle in the Bayfront Auditorium in Pensacola, every Sunday night, and as we only lived about 30 minutes drive away, we would get changed at home into our wrestling costumes. I would carry my bag, but it would only contain the gown I would wear for my entrance. As soon as my contest was over, I would go to the dressing room grab my bag, exit out of the stage door, drive home and get showered and cleaned up there. We always parked behind the Auditorium, near the stage door. I often wondered if anyone seeing us on our way to or from the Auditorium on a Sunday night, may have thought they were experiencing a 'close encounter,' as Gulf Breeze seemed to be the capital city for UFO sighting in those days.

The last time I remember confronting Beauty, the Beast and the Baroness in the Bayfront Auditorium, it turned out to be the wildest night yet. But, this time it was outside the ring. The weather that night was atrocious, and got worse by the minute. As usual, when we arrived at the venue, I drove around to the back of the building, which was on the pier facing out to sea. It wasn't just the driving wind and rain that was bad, but the waves were crashing over the end of the pier and almost flooding the back of the Auditorium itself. There was no way we could park our van in the usual spot, we were afraid it would get washed off the pier and out to sea. After driving back around the building, we found a spot to park on the land side of the building, then dashed through the weather into the front entrance. We found that in spite of the weather, the Auditorium was close to full. All the wrestlers were gathered in the dressing room at first, but as the weather deteriorated even further, we had to abandon it. We all feared that the ridiculously ferocious wind would blast the glass windows in. The torrential rain was being driven horizontally against them. The dressing room doors had to be closed, and all the other wrestlers got changed into their ring wear crowded together in the passageway that led to the ring area. Our contest, as usual was on last. By that time the usual roar of the fans was absolutely lost by the roar of the wind outside. There was a real concern that the building would blow away.

Now if that sounds like an exaggeration - get a load of this. As we were leaving the Auditorium we were met by a very distraught Baroness,

"COME AND LOOK AT THIS!!!!!!" She ordered us.

"Keep away from us," I warned her, "we are the enemy". we tried to keep our distance from the Baroness, as just minutes before, the fans had watched us at each other's throats. We followed her at a discreet distance, in order to find out what was wrong.

If we hadn't have seen this with our own eyes - I wouldn't have believed it. The Baroness had parked her Hot Pink Hearse on the pier well in front of the Auditorium, between two other vehicles. The wind had been so strong, that it had blown a large wooden, vendors kiosk, up into the air, and then dropped it like a bomb, vertically right down on top of the Baroness' Hot Pink Hearse. Although both the kiosk and the Hearse looked crushed, both the cars either side of hers, were totally unscathed. I wondered what her insurance company would make of that when she offered her explanation.

"Tell them it was an act of God." I suggested.

The feud that exploded onto The Continental scene was red hot - it was wilder than the weather was when the Baroness' Pink Hearse got crushed. Whenever I wrestled against Terry Garvin in single contests, all the other wrestlers would rush out of the dressing rooms to watch.

"DAMN - ADRIAN, WHAT DID YOU DO TO PISS YOU OFF SO BAD?!!!!' I was asked that question by the other wrestlers every time we fought. All the other wrestlers were certain that I was really trying to kill, or at least cripple The Beauty. A series of tag-team contests ended with disqualification for Beauty and the Beast, due to continual outside interference by The Baroness. We were not satisfied winning by disqualification, we wanted a decisive clear cut win. The Baroness had ambushed Linda a number of times, and Linda wanted revenge. We challenged The Beauty Garvin and The Baroness to fight us in a Mixed-Tag-team contest, in a Steel-Cage. The Beast, Marc

Gullen, was to be banned from ringside, and Todd Morton would lock the chain, that held the Steel door closed. He would then stand guard ringside. Well Linda was getting her revenge and then some. Even though the Baroness must have outweighed Linda by about 60 pounds, Linda pounded on the Female Ogre like she was an old War-Drum. Her broken arm, covered in rock hard plaster made a very formidable weapon. With Garvin and I, it was business as usual - I was ripping him from arsehole to breakfast time. Things were looking bad for the bad man and the bad girl -THEN - HERE COMES THE BEAST!!! The Beast came rushing down to ringside carrying a huge pair of BOLTCUTTERS!!! The fans screamed a warning - BUT TOO LATE! The Beast swung the Bolt-cutters over his head and brought them down onto Todd's head. Todd went out like a light, he hit the deck covered in BLOOD!

The Beast gave him a couple more whacks for good luck. Then he used the bolt-cutters to snap the chain securing the gate of the Steel Cage. The fans screamed a warning, but I was too busy battering Garvin. I had straddled him on the mat, and was beating out a drum message to some far distant tribe on his upturned mush. Linda didn't see him either, as she was too busy stomping on The Baroness. The Beast leapt into the ring swinging the Bolt-cutters. This time he brought them crashing down onto my head - that put me out of it. Linda was now at the mercy of The Baroness, Garvin and The Beast, who was armed with a huge pair of steel Bolt-cutters. Garvin slammed Linda onto the mat, then held her injured arm, while the Beast brought down the bolt-cutters repeatedly shattering the protective plaster to smithereens. Beauty, The Beast and The Baroness left the cage and marched back to the dressing room in triumph. They left Todd and I bleeding and Linda having to support her left arm with her right hand.

Beauty, The Beast and the Baroness had had their day - NOW I WANTED REVENGE!!!

Todd and I challenged Beauty and the Beast to a tag-match. A tag-match with special stipulations. It was a 'SPLIT THE TEAM' tag-match. Whichever team lost, would not be able to wrestle as a team again in the Continental area. Garvin and Gullen, flushed with their recent success, accepted our challenge enthusiastically. THE FIGHT WAS ON!

This might not have been for 'all the marbles,' but at least, it was for some of them. Garvin and Gullen marched triumphantly to the ring, as though they were already the victors. Gullen even sported an Exotically painted face, as though he was preparing himself to replace me. I could hardly contain myself waiting for the opening bell to sound. When it did, it was an all action WAR!!! No quarter was asked or given. It looked towards the end of the contest that I might lose the fall for our team. The Beast caught me in a crushing Bear hug, while Beauty climbed onto the top of their corner post. Then 'The Beast' hoisted me up facing his partner, and Garvin took an almighty leap, clothes-lining me right out of The Beast's arms. I had no sooner crashed backwards onto the mat, when Garvin grabbed me and hauled me back to my feet. He then held me securely in a Full-Nelson, while inviting his partner to do his worst. The Beast grabbed the huge bone that he had used to break Linda's arm. Then he climbed up onto the ropes. As Garvin held me in the Full-Nelson, The Beast dived into the air off the ropes, intending to bring the bone down onto my head. In a split second, I spun out of the Nelson, reversing our position. Now it was Garvin who took the massive blow from The Beast's big bone. Down he went and I dove onto him for the winning pinfall. The Beast attempted to break us up, but before he did, Todd Morton rushed across the ring from our corner and bowled the Beast arse over head, out of the ring. The referee continued his count - ONE - TWO - THREE!!! Beauty and the Beast were no longer tag-team partners. The look of shear shock registered on the faces of both our opponents was a treat to behold.

Garvin was absolutely hysterical. He rushed around the ring complaining and making every pathetic excuse he could think of, to MC Charlie Platt. Charlie showed the Sobbing Sissy no sympathy whatsoever. When he realized that his attempt had fallen on stony ground, he changed his tactics.

"Okay, Adrian," he pleaded into Charlie's microphone, "I can't lose my Beast. So I challenge you to a 'loser leaves town match. - But," he continued, "If you lose, you leave town, and me and my Beast can be tag-partners again! What do you say Adrian?!!!

"What do I say?" I replied, "Best offer I have had for years!"

Our contest was to be televised from Montgomery on their very next show. It was ACTION-ACTION-ACTION!!!! I bounced Garvin off every hard and sharp object I could find, both in and out of the ring. He did however manage a comeback and had me reeling for just a short while. But when he tried to capitalize on his advantage, he did so by attempting 'A Sleeping Beauty' which was Garvin's big special finish. Little did he know that I was expecting it, and as he dove in to deliver his coupe-de-grace - I ducked. Garvin sailed straight though the ropes and out of the ring. As he reentered the ring I caught him with a flying forearm smash, sending him crashing to the mat. I knew that I had really connected, and not wanting to lose my momentum I rushed in to finish him off. Then he dodged at the last second and I raced face first into the corner-post. As I bounced off and hit the mat, it gave Garvin an opportunity to fish out a pair of brass knuckles he had hidden in his tights. Unfortunately for him, unlike the referee, I had seen him do it. As I gained my feet, Garvin rushed in and threw a roundhouse at my face. I ducked the blow, which caused Garvin to spin around under his own momentum. I took full advantage by grabbing him and throwing him down onto his head and shoulders for another - ONE-TWO-THREE!!!!!

Well, I've got rid of 'The Garbage' - just onc Beast to go.

Now I challenged 'The Beast' Marc Gullen to a 'Loser leave town' Contest. I knew that in order to satisfy the fans, for all the foul and dastardly deeds perpetrated by the Beast, I would have to really do a lot more than just beat him and send him packing. This was the Animal that had injured Todd Morton, injured me, and had broken Linda's arm - TWICE!!! Well, when the night for REVENGE arrived, I made sure that I gave the fans everything they wanted, and then did it again for good measure. I was brutal and bestial, the Beast was bruised, battered and bloody. I gave the fans everything they wished for.

But - the old saying 'Be careful what you wish for,' could not have been more evident after I had got rid of 'Beauty' and 'The Beast.'

A movie, a wrestling territory, or a hero, is only as hot as their hottest villain. We might never of heard of David without Goliath. Where would Sherlock Holmes be without Moriarty? Who would have needed St George, if not for the Dragon?

The departure of our major nemesis, left a vacuum that couldn't be filled in time to make a difference. Robert Fuller who was booking/matchmaking attempted once again to top the bill, but he was boring and only a Star in his own mind. The lunatics had once again taken over the asylum and the Continental Wrestling Federation turned belly up - FOR GOOD!

LIFE IS LIKE A CAROUSEL

By now the rivalry between the WWF and the WCW had become so ridiculous that I began to lose interest. As a result I had began taking an interest again in art. As well as resuming painting in oils, I had began making framed base relief sculptures, and then painting them. The first base relief sculpture I created was a 19th century French Hussar riding on his dappled charger. I had always admired Circus/Carnival/Fairground art, so next I sculptured a Carousel Horse. Linda who loves all Horses, whether real or revolving on a Carousel, admired it and encouraged me to do more. We both became huge fans of the old, original carvers of these beautiful wooden antique masterpieces, and we began studying them. My favorites were Dentzel, Carmel - Looff, Muller, Illions, Parker's, Stein and Goldstein, Philadelphia Toboggan Company, I soon had quite a collection of my own creation. Mostly they were copies of the great old carvers, plus a few contemporary sculptures from my own imagination.

Our very good friends Ward Hall and Chris M. Christ used to exhibit their Carnival Freak Show at Pensacola Fairground every year. Their visits used to coincide with Linda's Birthday, and each year Chris would take Linda and I out for a meal to celebrate it. When Chris saw my collection of Carousel Sculptures, he told me there would be a good market for them. He suggested that I contact a friend of his, who had began auctioning Circus/Carnival/Fairground memorabilia and art at a yearly show in Tampa, Florida. I phoned Chris' friends Tommy Sciortino and Lynn Beckett and they invited Linda and I to exhibit our artwork as vendors at their auction. February 1990 we attended our first Circus/Carnival/Fairground show - it was AMAZING!

Tommy never charged us a vendor's fee. In fact he paid me to arrange the Carousel horses for viewing. I didn't actually move them myself, but was given a team of guys that placed each item where I decided it should go. It was there we met William Mann and his wife, who also became great friends. William was a photographer and author. His book 'Painted Ponies' is the best publication I have ever seen on Carousel Horses. My copy, autographed by William, is still on my bookshelf. I arranged many of the Horses in groups in front of huge colorful Circus banners, so that it would make very nice subjects for William to photograph. I got my own camera and followed him around taking almost identical photos for myself.

The undisputed STAR of the whole show, was a 'Parker Lilly-belle' that Tommy had recently purchased and restored, in order to auction at his show. He had removed all the old paint, right down to the wood grain. Then he had covered just the tail and the Horse's huge main with Gold leaf. It looked incredible. It was also an incredible success, and sold in the auction for a record breaking $88,000 plus. I took a photo of it which was also a success for me. I had it blown up to a 16" x 20" poster and it proved to be a best seller at all the future Carousel theme shows we attended. My best customer was Tommy. He must have bought dozens of them.

Small World - our very first customer of my Carousel Sculptures, was from Britain, and none other than Circus owner Jerry Cottrell. I wrestled under his big top on a number of occasions when Jacky Pallo promoted it. In spite of Pallo claiming to be his own BIG main draw, Jerry told me, that the only time his Circus tent sold out for wrestling, was when I wrestled in it.

As a result of our success at the Tampa Carousel Auction, we were invited to Mansfield, Ohio for their City's new Carousel Fest. Mansfield was the Home of The Carousel Works, where old antique Carousel figures are restored and new contemporary Carousel figures are carved. We were given a large studio in which to display our artwork. We shared the space with Beverly Price-Jones who hung her Pastel paintings in a small area at the back of the studio. Beverly's paintings were absolutely gorgeous. Beverly said the same about my artwork. She said that she would like to see what I could do with pastels. She brought out her big box of pastel crayons and a pad of paper. I must say, that my very first attempt at painting a Denzel Carousel Horse with pastels, was quite excellent. I became a fan and used pastels as well as oils to paint my pictures from that time on.

I was not particularly a fan of Carousel Menagerie Animals, but a Lady commissioned me to do a framed sculpture of a 'Dentzel Deer' which I copied from a photo of one that she owned. Although I only really like Carousel Horses, the Deer was such a success, that I did one for myself which I still possess.

Our trip to The Mansfield Carousel Exhibition turned out to be a great financial success. I remember telling Linda that I would like to become a full time artist - when I grew up.

We began receiving invites from all over. After attending a show in 'The Merry-go-Round Museum' in Sandusky, Ohio, the Museum purchased a number of my sculptures and paintings for their gift shop. When traveling through various towns en route to our next Carousel show, we often sold our art to various gift shops - although many of those were 'on commission.'

Next we went to Rochester N.Y. where we set up almost right next to the water in Lake Ontario Beach Park. Business there was okay, but the highlight of that trip was the beautiful 1905 Dentzel Carousel, that was housed in its own building close to the Lake. We found a private cheese and wine party, where we ate, drank and rode the Carousel until midnight quite delightful. It was there we met Bill Finkelstein who did a fantastic job of painting an otherwise fully restored antique Carousel Horse, while we watched. Bill also admired our artwork and invited us to visit 'The New England Carousel Museum' in Bristol Connecticut. We decided to drive there, beginning the next morning after the Lake Ontario Beach Park show was over. We made a B-line for Connecticut, and took in Buffalo, where we stayed the night. Next day we visited Niagara Falls, spending the first half of the day exploring Goat Island. SPECTACULAR - the last time I was that impressed, was the time I wadded two-thirds of the way across the top of Victoria Falls in Zambia, where I won my first World Championship. [see book 5 - 'Imagine what I could do to you.]

We both thought that 'The New England Carousel Museum' was FANTASTIC! We were also delighted to find that Bill Finkelstein had also booked us into a gorgeous private hotel, that used to be an exclusive Boys School at the turn of the century. It was almost like living in a comfortable, well furnished museum. The Lady who owned and ran the property was also a delight. Bill gave us an in-front and a behind-the-scenes tour of The Carousel Museum, and then almost floored us when he offered us both a fulltime job, working at the museum, restoring and repainting antique Carousel Horses.

Both Linda and I were seriously considering accepting Bill's job offer. We attended a number of actions at the museum, and their gift shop was for a time our very best customer for our artwork. Each time we journeyed to the museum's auction, we used it as a stepping stone to explore further north, New Hampshire and also Vermont, to view its glorious Autumn colors.

By now a year had passed since Linda and I had become obsessed with Carousel art. We had once again attended the Carousel auction in Tampa, West Palm Beach, and were now back in Mansfield, Ohio. This time we were going to set up in the newly opened 'Gail Guzzo Art Gallery.' We were given a huge room all to ourselves, that we were at first delighted with. Our enthusiasm soon evaporated, when we found that hardly anyone came to view our wares. The reason for that, we found was, that very few people even knew of the existence of the 'Gail Guzzo Gallery.' The entrance was just a small door that opened onto the street. In order to find Linda and I, one would have to enter the door, climb a dark stairway, then turn right into a dark passageway and walk through a couple of other large rooms, containing pieces of art, before they could find us. We just sat there for hours twiddling our thumbs, while all over Mansfield the Carousel Festival went merrily on without us. Next day we moved out of the Gallery and into 'The Carousel Works.' Things improved but not outrageously. Most people seemed more interested in our autographs than in our artwork. When I signed my name as 'Adrian Street,' I was asked if I could sign my autograph as 'Exotic' Adrian Street. Then we began to get interrupted by journalists and cameramen for the local newspapers.

This article by journalist Miriam Smith was written for 'Mansfield News Journal':

TOUGH WRESTLERS, DELICATE ARTISTS
Tag-team champs create fine Carousel carvings.

Mansfield - Artist Adrian Street delicately carves Carousel Horses. He also smashes faces and slams bodies in the big time wrestling ring.

"I guess I do a lot of sculpting in the ring because there's a lot of ugly wrestlers, and I beat them until they look pretty." Street said with a devilish grin.

He and his wife, Linda Street are exhibiting their Carousel Art this weekend during the second annual Mid-West Carousel Exhibition in Downtown Mansfield. The exhibit opens Friday from 11am to 5.30 pm and runs through Sunday at The Guzzo Gallery. The Streets will be at the opening to greet art or wrestling buffs.

It's no wonder the Streets are so intrigued by Carousel creatures that merrily spin around - this tag-team duo makes a lot of heads spin around in the ring. 'Exotic' Adrian Street and Miss Linda, as their stage names go, are the World Mixed Tag-team Wrestling Champions. Street also said he has been World Champion in three different weight divisions.

The spandex clad Husband and Wife team discussed their diverse interests recently while relaxing in The Guzzo Gallery. The Streets are originally from England and now live in Gulf Breeze, Florida.

"We're cutting back on our wrestling to concentrate on our artwork." said Street in a heavy English accent.

His Carousel sculptures reflect his commitment. The wooden creatures sparkle with bright vibrant colors and intricate designs. He said creating the Carousel animals is basically a three step process -sculpting, painting and framing. Street uses virtually every medium he can get his hands on to make them sparkle.

Street said he's always been fascinated with Carousel Figures. A year ago, a friend who runs a Freak show tipped him off about the popularity of Carousel Art.

Gail Guzzo, director and owner of Guzzo Gallery, praised Street's use of colors.

"Aside from the obviously very colorful images that Adrian uses, in my opinion there's an apparent positive and negative use of tones," Guzzo said.

Street said his artwork is hanging in 'The Estate Gallery' in Pensacola, Florida. Some of his artwork is being shown in the Soviet Union as part of a cultural exchange. Though he's pleased that his artwork is being recognized, Street said he gets the most pleasure out of his Carousel creations.

"I think there's some sort of magic about these things," said Street, who has Indian paintings on display. "Nobody really grows up."

Mrs. Street also will be exhibiting her Carousel Horses, which sparkle with glitter and beads. She said her fascination with Horses is nothing new,

"I'm nuts about Horses, so anything to do with Horses I go potty about." she said.

En route to Mansfield for the Carousel Exhibition, The Streets participated in two wrestling matches - which they won.

Initially we had both been very enthused - excited even, at the prospect of working for Bill Finkelstein at 'The New England Carousel Museum' but I imagined that once the novelty had worn off it would just be a 'job.' Also Bristol, Connecticut was okay, but I didn't want to live there. We loved Gulf Breeze in Florida.

The two wrestling matches which the newspaper referred took place in Madison, Wisconsin. It was there that I wrestled first against 'The White Angel' and then against an old friend, Big Billy Anderson. It was so very refreshing to wrestle with such an excellent opponent. It made me realize just how much I had missed wrestling. Wrestling was in my blood and always would be. Billy could wrestle in the old style that I had always loved. He told me that he and referee Jesse Hernandez had opened a wrestling school - 'The School of Hard Knocks,' and were teaching young pupils the old style - the good style - the right style of wrestling. - There was hope for the wrestling business after all, I thought.

SKULLKRUSHER'S WRESTLING SCHOOL

As fate would have it, I wrestled on a show about 30 miles away from my home, promoted by 'Wild Samoan' Seca. It was in a nearby Air-force base. I wrestled another good hard contest against 'Iceman' King Parsons. While there, I made friends with a young officer who told me that he would like to learn to wrestle. I told him that Seca had a wrestling school that he operated somewhere in Pensacola. He insisted that he wanted to learn properly, and didn't think that Seca would do him much good. He then suggested that he and I could open a school, and share the proceeds. He came to my house a week or so later and told me that he had found a suitable building that we could rent for just over $3,000 a month. I must admit that I didn't warm to that plan at all - the rent would still have to be paid whether the school attracted students or not. Then we would have to furnish the place with a ring and exercise equipment. Also I couldn't see what advantage it would be, to share proceeds with someone who didn't know anything about wrestling. I remembered thinking how great it was, that guys like Billy Anderson and Jesse Hernandez were teaching young wrestlers the right way. I decided to do it too - alone. I also decided, to erect a building myself. There was no room where we lived, in The Bahama Bay Club, so we gave up that property and moved back into one of my apartments. There, there was a large garden at the back of the property where I could erect a suitable building. Also there were three other apartments so that when each became vacant, I could use them to house our out of town student wrestlers. We called our wrestling school 'Skullkrushers.'

I built the ring inside as part of the building. I lined one whole wall with mirrors, where I installed all the weights and exercise equipment. Beside the building I had an above ground swimming pool built. On top of the school building, I built a gazebo in one corner that I planted with various types of climbing flowers. There was also beds for sunbathing, a barbeque, tables and chairs. A beautiful roof garden on top of my Wrestling School. It was great.

Our first ever students were a Brother and Sister, who were a real life gimmick. Janet was 28 years old and stood 4 feet 6 inches tall. James was 16 years old, stood 6 feet 8 inches and weighed well over 400 pounds. Janet wanted to be trained as James' valet and wanted to be named Miss J.R. James wanted to be named 'The Lord of Pain'. James was a monster in size, but had a plump, red 16 year old face. Thank goodness he wanted to wear a mask. The rest of his outfit consisted of leather, Studs and chains. I must say that their costumes transformed them from two cartoon characters, into - well cartoon characters with a sinister edge. For a few days they had a whole apartment to themselves. Then my sister Pam, her husband Mike, Daughter Teena and Teena's fiancé. Then out of the blue my eldest son Adrian Jr. turned up with a friend. Our student's apartment and our own, almost burst at the seams.

After my family returned to Britain, the Lord of Pain and Miss J.R. were not alone for long. Our next student was Dave Lewis. I first met Dave when he began promoting shows in Dothan, Alabama. His first persona was 'The Knight Templar.' Eventually he changed into 'The American Warrior. We were then hit with an avalanche of students from everywhere, Canada, Australia, Germany, Sweden, Belgium, The Caribbean, Canada, Britain and of course from all over the United States.

I could easily write a whole book about various wrestling students, I won't though, as I think I'll leave it for them to write their own books one day.

Soon after I had opened 'Skullkrushers' I received a phone call from the 'Boogie-Woogie-man' Jimmy Valiant,

"Hey Brother," he growled, "I've just taken a page out of your book."

"What have you done Jimmy," I asked, "Have you started wearing lipstick?"

"No not that," he laughed, "I've opened a wrasslin' school - I'm teachin' wrasslin.'"

"Well Jimmy," I replied, "You can do something for your wrestling students that I can't do for mine."

"What's that?" he asked.

"You can teach them everything you know about wrestling in less than two minutes." I told him. Although Jimmy really didn't know anything about wrestling, he was a great character, very entertaining and in spite of his shortcomings, I still thought he was an asset to the business.

WWF

I have been asked more times than I can recall, why I was never asked to work for the WWF. Well actually I was asked.

In spite of all the many substandard doppelgangers created by Vince's mob, it seemed they didn't want the genuine article. They had an entirely different image in mind for me. I wasn't even going to be a wrestler - I guessed that Vince didn't want anything he didn't understand - like wrestling! Even before their title was changed to the WWE, Vince was not running a wrestling promotion. He had turned his Father's Wrestling promotion into a 'TV Reality Show,' with little emphasis on 'REALITY.' If most of his top 'Superstars' had been hung for being wrestlers, they would have died innocent.

When he did have access to great wrestlers, he, or his script writers, thought up the most goofy and belittling personas for them. Two prime examples he turned one great wrestler Matt Borne into 'Doink the Clown. Another great wrestler, Terry Taylor into a fucking chicken. As 'The Red Rooster' complete with a dyed scarlet topknot on his head, Terry's new role was to cuckle, crow and run around flapping his elbows. Terry was a WRESTLER and should be respected as such!!!

Anyway, back to my case. I would not be cast as a wrestler either, they wanted me to act as a Manager for a British Tag-Team. I had no problems with that at all, especially when I thought of the kind of money that I'd heard that could be made in the WWF. Plus - the World wide exposure that the WWF enjoyed, could do me nothing but good - or so I thought.

I was more than ready to swap my gaudy wrestling wear, for whatever garb my new Manager's image suggested - until I learned what that image would be. The two British wrestlers I was scheduled to manage were to be 'The British Skinheads' and I was to be their over the top 'NEO-NAZI MANAGER!!!!!!!!!!!!!!'

STICK THAT RIGHT UP YOUR ARSE VINCE!!!!

I had been born in Britain in 1940 - I grew up while the Nazis were bombing my country into dust. I remember seeing newsreels of the Nazi Death-camps.

I loved seeing pictures of various members of the Human Race, I didn't hate any of them. I am happy and willing to respect anyone and what they stand for, as long as that respect is mutual. I am not a racist and never will be - that very much includes posing as one for a comic cuts organization.

I had been WRESTLING PRO since 1957 when I was 16 years old. I was now past my 51st Birthday. I was very proud of my legacy as a professional wrestler, the persona that the WWF had in mind for me was without a doubt insulting, and the worse possible image that I would have thought of, during my worst nightmare. So now you know why I have PROUDLY NEVER WORKED FOR THE WWF.

At that time one of my own former managers J.J. Dillon was working for the WWF, he phoned me on their behalf, and asked me if I wouldn't reconsider their offer.

I DON'T THINK THEY'LL CALL AGAIN FOR A WHILE!!!!!

NATURE BOY BUDDY ROGERS

On the 26th of June 1992, one of my all time favorite wrestlers died. 'Nature Boy' Buddy Rogers, directly or indirectly, helped to shape my wrestling persona more than any other wrestler on the Planet. When I attempted to emulate him, after writer, Charles Mascall had dubbed me 'Nature-Boy' Adrian Street, my fortunes in Pro Wrestling took a mighty upward swing. Just a few years before his demise, I had first met Buddy and we had become great friends. I was both amazed and delighted, that many of Buddy's wrestling stories ran parallel to many of my own. In Buddy's own words - 'He was often imitated - never duplicated.'

The incident that led to Buddy's demise, would have been comical if it hadn't been so tragic. He was shopping in his local Supermarket, when he was recognized by a Lady who had been a great fan of his for decades. She ran up to him and asked for his autograph. In her haste, and shaking with excitement as she tried to extract a pen and paper from her handbag. In so doing, she dropped a cheesecake she had just put in her shopping basket onto the floor. After signing his autograph for the Lady and saying goodbye, he decided to treat her to his famous 'Nature-Boy' Strut. Unfortunately mid strut, he stepped on the cheesecake she had dropped, and took a big unscheduled bump. He landed elbow first and chipped it very badly. The pain was so bad, that just a few days later he had a heart attack and died.

In my opinion, Buddy was one of the greatest professional wrestlers ever.

****

A very strange contest took place in a venue in Mississippi. Linda and I had already had our contest, and were now watching a match between 'Wildcat' Wendall Cooley and a local boy. It was a strange contest because Wendall was used to being the good guy in all his matches. The fact that on that night he was wrestling against a local boy, made him very unpopular. The fans booed Wendall and cheered his opponent - something Wendall was not at all used to. The more the fans booed and jeered the more aggressive Wendall became. Soon, he was being regarded as the villain. Some of the local boy's friends really became verbally aggressive, then they began to challenge Wendall. Wendall retaliated by inviting them to come into the ring and try their luck. One of them did. Wendall grabbed him as he came through the ropes, and was controlling him handily. BUT, referee Ronnie West got over excited and punched the guy in the face as Wendall was holding him. BIG MISTAKE - it seemed that almost everyone in the audience leapt out of their seats and began to invade the ring. But, before a single one of them made contact with Wendall, Linda shot off as though she had been fired from a cannon. Before one irate fan laid a fist on Wendall, Linda beat them to the punch. The very second Linda had taken off, I was right behind her and the second to enter the ring, to reinforce Wendall and Ronnie West. We were punching, kicking, slamming fans back out of the ring almost as fast as they were pilling in. As more and more hostile fans invaded the ring, they were opposed by more wrestlers filling out of the dressing room and into the fray. In no time the Police began to invade the ring too. - Time to piss off!

Linda and I were already changed into our street clothes, so we left the building as soon as we could. As I drove out of the building, and onto the road, I almost immediately met a road block. There was a huge fire truck blocking the road with Police cars and uniformed officers everywhere. I covered my hair, with the hood on my jacket, before rolling down the window and asking what the problem was. There had been a riot in the wrestling venue, we were informed.

"Oh - how awful!" I responded. Then they backed the fire truck enough so that I could drive by. I couldn't believe our luck at not being recognized. Only minutes earlier, Linda and I had been right in the thick of the riot. We were lucky, as we learned the next night that the rest of the wrestlers had been held up for hours by the Police. Wendall came very close to smashing Danny Davis' face, as he was the only wrestler there that night, who didn't rush to Wendall's aid. Wendall told me that, even though he had his hands full at the time, he had spied Danny Davis, watching what was happening in the ring from a table that he had set up to sell his souvenir photos from. He was only a few seconds from the ring, but cowered there, too frightened to lend a hand.

THE UNDEAD

The Baroness called us and told me that she was working for a small time promoter who ran a weekly venue near Panama City, about 90 miles from where we lived. He had asked her to phone me, to ask if I would wrestle for him. He offered reasonable wages, so I agreed to. When we arrived at the venue we found that it was an enormous corrugated metal structure, that was normally used for repairing motor vehicles. When we entered we found that it was packed like a can of Sardines with wrestling fans. The promoter was also his own main event, and wrestled as yet another version of the macabre 'Dr. Death'. The Baroness was his Macabre Vampire like valet. Although he was the promoter, the good Doctor appreciated that I would not ever allow him to score a victory over me. What he did request, was the favor that I would allow him to last at least 20 minutes before I beat him.

"No problem," I assured him, "and if you want your pet Vampire to interfere, to help you get more heat, that's fine too." I found that they were ahead of me in that aspect. When my fanfare sounded I entered the ring. When my fanfare ended the Baroness grabbed the microphone, introduced Dr. Death and then drew my attention to her coffin, which she had placed on a table ringside. The purpose of the coffin, she explained, was there to place me in, after her wrestler, Dr. Death had finished mauling me to death. Well Dr. Death turned out to have the distinction of being the most unfit, out of condition, wrestlers I have ever stepped into the ring with. He was gasping and wheezing within two minutes of action. Before we had battled for five minutes, he was begging me to finish the contest. BUT - I had promised him at least 20 minutes - it was the main event, and in spite of a semi-lifeless villain, the fans were cheering like crazy, and did not deserve to be short changed. The Baroness had been squawking threats from ringside since before the contest had began. So, in order to give Dr. Death a chance to get his breath back, I responded to her. We spent a couple of minutes engaged in a verbal battle, then I went back to work on Dr. Death.

"FINISH IT - FINISH IT!" He croaked. Instead, I walked back across the ring in response to the Baroness' latest barrage of threats and warnings. Dramatically she threw open the hinged lid of the coffin, and again told me that she would soon be placing me into it, and nailing it down - just as soon as her wrestler Dr. Death had finished with me. I couldn't resist looking over to where Dr. Death was still laying in the corner wheezing like an early prototype of Stevenson's Rocket. I looked at the fans - sighed and raised my eyebrows, and they exploded with laughter in response.

"YOU WILL BE NAILED IN HERE VERY SOON!!!" The Baroness screeched a promise, while pointing inside the open coffin. I leapt out of the ring, scooped up the Baroness and slammed her into her own coffin. After slamming down the lid, I jumped onto the table, then onto the coffin, and then called for them to play my entrance music. While the music played - and hopefully my opponent recovered, I sang and danced on the lid of the coffin that contained the Vampire Baroness. When 'Imagine what I could do to you,' finished playing, I leapt back into the ring to continue my life and death battle with Dr. Death.

"FINISH IT!!!" was all I got out of him - so I did.

It was a long time before she ever spoke to me again. I didn't know it, and I never would have guessed, but the Baroness' greatest fear was of small dark spaces.

That was a night to remember, Dr. Death was dying of asphyxiation and his valet was a claustrophobic Vampire.

LADIES

There were a number of promotions who specialized in Ladies Wrestling that Linda wrestled for. For those our roles were reversed and I became Linda's Manager/valet. One of these was F.L.A.I.R. based in Hollywood, Florida. F.L.A.I.R. was hosted by Joe Pedicino and Boni Blackstone, they both commented on the contests from ringside. Linda wrestled with a number of opponents, but the very best by far was Debbie Combs. That match could have been a main event in any arena in the World. After a hard fought contest it ended in a time-limit draw after both contestants double clotheslined each other seconds before the bell sounded.

The other Ladies promotion was the L.P.W.A. and was televised in a Casino in Laughlin, Nevada. We would fly to Las Vegas where a private bus would pick us up at the airport, and then drive us to the venue. The wages were excellent, but damn, the Girls really had to earn it. We would stay at the same casino for two days and nights each trip. The Girls would perform in about four different shows in one day. Amongst Linda's various opponents was Candi Devine, who wrestled in a mask as 'The Goddess.' We called her 'The Dogess.' Other Masked opponents were 'Devilla' and 'El Gato.' who Linda wrestled a couple of times each. Susan Sexton who Linda had wrestled previously in Germany and in Britain, was the new L.P.W.A. Ladies Champion. There were many excellent contestants including Leiani Kai, Judy Martin, Bambi, Malia Hosaka. Reggie Bennett who Linda and I had first met when we all starred in 'Grunt the Wrestling Movie.' Reggie wrestled as 'Big Mo.' Her tag-partner 'Little Mo' was Cheryl Rusa. Cheryl really was tiny. Linda and I more or less adopted her. We took her training with us each morning in a gym that we found on the other side of the Colorado River from the casino. She might have been tiny but she was really strong - especially for someone so elflike.

Wendi Richter, was there, also Medusa Micheli, Susan Green, Sheba 'The Desert Rose', Sindy Paradise, Lisa Star, Nasty Kat La

Roux, Nasty Linda Dallas, Misty Blue Simms, Heidi Lee Morgan, Alison Royal, Comrade Olga Stalinska, Peggy Lee Leather wrestled as 'Lady X.' There was Magnificent Mimi, Tina Moretti, Yukai Osaka, Sweet Georgia Brown, Rockin' Robin, and many more. The announcers included Jim Cornett, Joe Pedicino, Nick Bockwinkle, Sgt. Slaughter and Ken Resnik.

In a contest against Leiani Kai, Linda didn't only have her to contend with, but was attacked and blindsided over and over again by Judy Martin, who was Leiani Kai's manager that night. Every time Linda rallied and came back at her, Judy Martin would grab, trip, kick, or punch her to turn things back in their favor. It was only after Judy Martin dragged Linda outside the ring, where both she and Leiani beat on her, hoisted her up and slammed her, that I rushed around the ring and abruptly brought the contest to an end. I grabbed Leiani and Judy and slammed their heads together. That was one hectic battle!

Boogaloo Brown as manager of 'Bad, Black and Beautiful' had an humongous amount of heat on him. This was due to his skullduggery and continual interference during contests on his team's behalf. All the fans were incensed with the desire to see him massacred. Now any villain with that kind of heat, could only maintain that kind of heat by constantly denying the fans the fulfillment of their desire. When Linda was wrestling one of his stable, Boogaloo got tremendous heat, when he continually attempted to trip, punch, or distract her. Obviously, as Linda's manager, I would take an extremely dim view of his antics. The fans wanted and expected me to take Boogaloo - RIP HIS HEAD OFF AND MAKE HIM EAT IT!!! BUT - you can't have heroes unless you have VILLAINS - MONSTERS or GIANTS to slay. None of those - then a hero becomes redundant. So I told Boogaloo before the contest began,

"WHATEVER YOU DO - DON'T LET ME CATCH YOU!!!" I explained to him, that if I chased him and caught him, the fans would expect me to destroy him. If I did, then he would lose all his heat, and there would be one less Big Bad Wolf in the woods. Beating up on Boogaloo Brown would not have been anything to boast about. He was not even as big as me, and he was not a wrestler. After all I had explained to him, Boogaloo choose to ignore my advice. When Linda was beating on one of his stable, while she held her over the ropes, Boogaloo grabbed Linda by the hair and almost pulled her out of the ring by it. I raced to the rescue. SO - what did Boogaloo do? Well he didn't run like I told him to - HE TRIED TO FIGHT ME OFF!!!! I trampled him like a herd of Bison,

"RUN FOR IT!!!" I strongly suggested to him, as I scooped him off the ground and nutted him in the gob. He ignored my suggestion.

I smacked him in the chops so hard my hand stung for the rest of the day.

"PISS OFF!!!" I told him, in no uncertain manner. The only excuse I could think of, for his blatant stupidity, was the glazed eyes and slack jaw. I wondered if he was still conscious. Well all the audience had wanted to see Boogaloo get his comeuppance and they were getting it big time. I finally left him where I slammed him, after doing a shithouse shuffle from his head to his toes.

In another of Linda's contests, I leapt into the ring to avenge an attack on her, when the suave, but villainous, Shaven headed, Jonathan Blue, attempted to take a little unfair advantage. I had never heard of Jonathan Blue before, and I don't think he was ever a wrestler, but when I charged across the ring and WHACKED HIM - he took one of the best big bumps over the ropes that I had ever seen. Very impressive indeed - good one Jonathan Blue..

The World Mixed-Tag-team titles that Linda and I had won in Germany in the mid 70s from Don Kovaks and Suzie Parker, was recognized by the L.P.W.A. and we were asked to defend those titles against a couple of other teams. The most notable was a title contest between Linda and myself against Sheba 'The Desert Rose' and her manager, wrestler Sheik Adnan Al-Kaissie. Adnan was from Bagdad, in Iraq and had been a classmate and friend of future Iraqi Dictator Saddam Hussein.

He stood 6 feet and weighed 255 pounds. It the Giant Al-Shaab Stadium in Bagdad he defeated Andre the Giant in front of a sellout crowd.

I first met him in Britain when he wrestled there as Red Indian, Billy White Wolf. We had become instant friends and I was very happy to meet up with him again after so many years.

Unfortunately, for whatever reason, my feelings were not reciprocated, and I found him very surly and unfriendly. Also he seemed to think that Sheba and he should become the new Mixed Tag-team World Champions.

"Not much chance of that." I told him. He made no reply - he didn't have to, the look he gave me said it all.

I told Linda before we entered the ring to be very careful, and not to let Sheba put her in any compromising positions,

"If she does anything dodgy at all," I warned Linda, "take her out!" Turned out I had no worries there, they were having a good contest. "Tag me in!" I called to Linda, I wanted to find out what The Iraqi had in mind. I was happy now that I was aware of his crappy attitude, if he had been more friendly in the dressing room, I could have easily been lulled into a sense of false security.

Linda and I were 'the good guys' in this contest, which really put me at a disadvantage. As a good guy, the fans would expect me to instigate the action. I always like it better when the ball is in my opponent's court. Well I didn't have to contemplate my dilemma for long. For a big man, he could move and was in my face in a flash. We grappled for a while, I remained mostly on the defensive, learning all the time what he intended to do. Eventually, I relaxed enough to allow him to apply something he seemed to be trying for since the get go. As we faced each other he trapped both of my arms with his and attempted to move me to an area in the ring where he could best perform his intended maneuver. OOOOOPS!!! I could feel a very distinct Suplex coming my way!!! Having forgotten to pack my parachute, I decided to cancel my flight. Instead I swung us both around and back against the ropes. We both took turns with our backs against the ropes as he struggled to get me into a better position for 'take off!'

"Loosen up!" he growled.

"Fuck off!" I replied. I managed to move my trapped right arm around thanks to our sweaty bodies and placed my hand under the Iraqi's chin and pushed his head up and back. He pushed back with all his might. I suddenly took my hand away. As his head shot forward, I threw my own forward with equal force. As I was a lot shorter, the tip of my forehead crashed into the big man's nose. At the same time I managed to slide my slippery arms free, stepped around and flung him over my hip onto the canvas. I held him down in a headlock, easily controlling him in spite of his frantic struggling. Linda finished the contest with a display of much better action than the Iraqi and I had displayed. We emerged from the ring the same way we entered it - as the UNDEFEATED MIXED TAG-TEAM CHAMPIONS OF THE WORLD.

AROUND THE WORLD IN 8 DAYS

I received a phone call from a TV station in Japan. They wanted me to fly out there to appear on one of their shows. We were so very busy with our costumes at that time, that I really didn't have the time to spare. As I didn't really want to go, I decided to demand a sum for my appearance that would dampen their enthusiasm.

"I wouldn't be able to make that trip for less than $10,000." I told them.

"No problem." They replied.

Damn it, I still didn't want to go.

"Where will I stay while I'm in Tokyo?" I asked, hoping I could pick fault with their choice of bed and bode.

"The 'Akasaka Prince Hotel." They told me.

I certainly couldn't complain about that. Back to the drawing board.

"I will have to fly first class." I warned them.

"No problem." They replied.

Damn, it seemed that they wouldn't refuse any request I made. I suddenly had a flash of inspiration. I wondered if I could use this trip to visit friends and family in Britain.

"If I agree to come, I want an open First Class ticket from the States to Tokyo. Then from Tokyo to London, and then from London back to the States."

"No problem." They replied.

Looks like I'm going to Japan. As I mentioned, Linda and I were really busy with our costume making and the wrestling school. It was because of that, that we decided that Linda would stay and take care of business, and I would take the trip alone. That was a decision that I regret to this day. I saw and experienced so many things that would have meant a thousand times more, if I had shared them with Linda.

Linda drove me to Pensacola airport, from there I flew to Atlanta. From Atlanta to Anchorage, Alaska and then on to

Tokyo, Japan, it was all First Class. That was even better than the chartered flight I had been on, that took me from Scotland to Nairobi where I played a Neolithic Cannibal in the movie 'Quest for fire.'

After I eventually alighted in Tokyo, I was met at the airport and chaffered to the Akasaka Prince Hotel. On our journey from the airport into Tokyo, I was thrilled to see Mount Fuji in the distance, and then astonished at the sheer size of a building that my driver described as 'The Indoor Winter Olympic training centre.' They had everything in there he boasted, even a full sized Ski Slope.

During my very, very long flight, I had eaten a ton of delicious food, and drank a bath full of excellent wine. I hadn't been asleep for more than a day and by now it was really beginning to catch up with me. AND my ordeal had just began. The moment I stepped into the Hotel, I was met by a crowd of TV personnel, all of whom wanted to go over what my role was to be in their show. A show which was due to commence in just a few more hours time. I was absolutely exhausted.

My room was fantastic. I could lay in bed with a remote in my hand, press a button of my choice, not only to turn the TV off and on, and change the channels, but I could turn the lights on and off, make them dimmer or brighter. I could also press a button to open and close the curtains on the windows of which two sides of that beautiful room comprised. My room must have been very close to the top of the building, from my wall to wall windows, I could look out to a vast panoramic view right over Tokyo. In the wardrobe was a selection of Kimonos that I could wear in order to be as comfortable as possible. How I missed having Linda with me. I had a very large refrigerator in the room. It was stocked with miniature bottles of every kind of spirit and liquor I had ever seen and a lot that were brand new. I didn't touch one single drop. If I had, there would have been no TV show for me in just a few more hours time. I looked longingly at the EMPEROR sized bed. I decided against that too. If I went to bed now, they wouldn't get me out of it till tomorrow. Instead I drank a couple of bottles of ice cold water then went out into the streets of Tokyo to explore and walk.

A chauffeured Limo came to the hotel to take me to the TV studio, where I was introduced to two young Ladies who would be my interpreters. I was shown to my 'Star' dressing room, that had the title of my part of the show written in Japanese and English beside the door. 'The Exotic World of Wrestling.' I checked out the set before the studio audience began entering, and was both surprised and delighted by what I saw. There was a colored photo of my head and shoulders, wearing my most colorful regalia, which was so massive that it filled one entire wall of the studio. Every person I met in Japan seemed so polite, that I hoped I didn't appear to be too barbaric in comparison.

Before I made my entrance, they showed a video of a number of very butch Japanese wrestlers, smashing each other to pieces. Then by contrast they ran a contest between Jackie Pallo Jr. and I, that had taken place in Florida. I could tell straight away, by the audience's reaction, that I was going to be a hit. 'Imagine what I could do to you,' was played at full blast to herald my entrance. It seemed that I was a 'surprise guest' and when they saw me, the audience came apart. The show went great, all I did was be 'EXOTIC!' I teased every other person on the set, which delighted the studio audience, who reacted as though I was the World's most famous Rock Star. I sat next to Beat Takeshi Kitano, who was a comedian/writer/producer/artist and actor. According to my Son, Adrian Jr. who later saw the video of the show, told me Beat was also Japan's biggest Action movie Star. Japan's answer to Clint Eastwood.

After the show, when we were leaving the building, there were crowds of fans waiting for me - I mean the whole street was packed like a giant can of sardines. I had only seen the likes, when 'The Beatles' tried to leave stadiums after their concerts. We managed to get to our vehicle, and then nudged our way through the crowd. It really was quite surreal. From the studio I was taken to a fantastic restaurant where I enjoyed my very first taste of 'Kobe Steak.' DELICIOUS - But maybe too tender for my very strong teeth. Japan was amazing - my big regret was that Linda was not with me.

From the time I had left Atlanta, Georgia I had been traveling West through numerous time zones, and by now I had completely lost my concept of time. Give or take, I think I must have been in

Japan for about three days. After again flying West from Tokyo to London, I became even more confused. Chronic lack of sleep didn't help.

After arriving in Britain, I took the tube train from Heathrow to Victoria Station, where my old Wrestling buddy, Tony Scarlo had agreed to pick me up. Just as the train began to move out of Heathrow, I became aware of just about everyone in the compartment staring at me. Then a man addressed me, asking

"Excuse me - but didn't you used to be Adrian Street, the wrestler?"

"Yes, and I still am - last time I looked." I replied. Then it seemed as though a dam had collapsed, as everyone in the compartment began to crowd around me asking me for autographs and telling me about when they had seen me wrestle on TV, and who I was wrestling. I was really quite amazed that everyone remembered me so well, as at that time, I had not wrestled on British TV for almost 20 years. I wonder what gave me away?!

I met Tony outside Victoria Station and he drove me to his home, where I would be staying with him and his Wife Rose while in London. Just beyond a swimming pool that Tony had in his back garden, he had a great little gym. As exhausted as I was, the feel of a heavy barbell in my hands always helped to rejuvenate me. Tony took me to 'Winnie' Bill Bridges pub, we had a drink and a laugh - just like old times. Then he took me to Portobello Road Antique Market - a favorite haunt of mine from the very first time I visited London. On the way back to Tony's home, he stopped his car and asked me if I recognized where I was. I told him I didn't have a clue. Then he shocked me, when he told me that we were parked directly opposite to where 'Dale Martin's' Wrestling Promotions Offices used to be. Even after he told me, it was almost impossible to imagine that that is where I was. Everything had changed so much.

The next morning I took a train on my own to London's West end. I explored and noticed very little had changed since I had lived there. I had phoned my kids and arranged to meet them in my all time favorite Vegetarian' restaurant 'Cranks.' I got there first and waited for their arrival. It was great to see Adrian, Vince and Mandy again, and also meet some new faces that I had never before met in person. There was Vince's Wife, Shane, with their son, my Grandson, nine year old Gary. Then there was Mandy and Mandy's husband John, and their Daughter, my Granddaughter, 14 month old Chloe. Two really good looking Grandchildren. Gary was bright and cheerful, Baby Chloe was absolutely gorgeous. Once again I wished that Linda was with me to meet everyone. We had a meal together in 'Cranks' before window shopping our way to Oxford Street, then all the way down to Marble Arch. We walked through Hyde Park and ended up sitting and chatting next to the Serpentine. By the time we retraced our steps back up Oxford Street, we were all hungry again. We decided on a big Pizza Restaurant. Nine year old Gary, who seemed to want to show off his reading skills while browsing the menu, announced that he would have 'Cream Spong.' Well that was the way he pronounced Sponge. That made Adrian laugh so much, that even today he calls Gary 'Spong-Boy.' After a bottle or two of red grape blood, my trip this far around the World was once more chiming its toll. We all parted company outside Tottenham Court Road underground Station. The kids travelled back to Milton Keynes, and I to Tony Scarlo's home. By the time I arrived there, I was seeing double. Then Tony announced that my Sister Pam had called him earlier and demanded that I visit them in Wales before I returned home to Florida.

"You'll have to come and fetch me." I told her. They would have got lost in London, looking for Tony's home, so Tony drove me to Heathrow Airport, where we met them. Pam's husband Mike was driving. It seemed surreal driving through the early hours of the morning, along old roads that I had frequented so often in the many years gone by. As we arrived at Pam and Mike's home, it was just getting light enough to make out the massive Milfraen Mountain that loomed dominantly and eternally over Brynmawr. It seemed that I had barely closed my eyes, when I was awakened and told that an old friend had come to see me. It was 'Mr. South-Wales' himself, Colin Thomas. I first met Colin in Brynmawr's Swimming pool in 1956. I was 15 years old at that time, and very much into Bodybuilding. Colin was ten years older and a champion bodybuilder. When I'd asked him if he was Colin Thomas, he replied,

"Yes I am - how big do you think my chest is?" I found that all these years later, Colin's attitude had hardly changed. I had taken my camera on my round the World trip, so naturally, I wanted a few photos of me with one of my very first training partners.

I gave the camera to Pam, And intended placing my arm around Colin's shoulder for the photo. Before I had a chance, Colin had whipped of his shirt,

"Let's give them a double biceps Ade!" he grunted, "Then we'll give them a side chest!" As I said - Colin's attitude had not changed at all.

I had an early flight from London to Atlanta, Georgia. We arrived early at the airport, and had time for a good old fashion 'English Breakfast' before I got boarded. We had a photo taken of that too. Finally I arrived back in Pensacola, and was met there by Linda, who was there to take me home. Of all the photos I had to show Linda of my very exotic trip, the ones that made her the most envious was the photos of 'The old fashioned English breakfast.' Now that's Linda for you.

It took me days to readjust to the time - I could never really work out how long I had spent in any of each of the countries I had visited, but was now able to work out that I had gone 'Around the World in 8 days'.

****

Back at Skullkrushers my students were enthusiastic and very much ready to go. I've always maintained, that you could not be too enthusiastic, when it came to learning the art of professional wrestling - BUT!!!!! I told my students that I would spend so many hours with them each day. We would usually begin by lifting weights before getting into the ring. Then we would wrestle - wrestle - wrestle. When I was finished for the day, I would tell them they could practice amongst themselves as long as they wanted. The ring and the weights were there for them to use 24 hours a day if they wanted. I warned them not to attempt any wrestling moves that I had not yet taught them. Then I would tell them that we would resume our lessons tomorrow morning.

I would then leave them after telling them that Linda and I now wanted the evening for ourselves. BUT - I might be half way through dinner, or watching one of my favorite shows on TV, when BANG - BANG - BANG!!! on the door, I'd open it and -

"ADRIAN - COULD YOU SHOW US HOW TO PUT A FIGURE-FOUR LEG-LOCK ON AGAIN - I DON'T THINK WE'RE DOING IT RIGHT!!!"

This was not an isolated incident this was a regular occurrence. Living so close to our student wrestlers was driving me nuts - I loved them all - but I needed my space.

We began looking for a quiet peaceful home, where we could be completely on our own, when lessons were over for the day. We found a Log-cabin that was ideal. All you could see of the property from the road was a narrow driveway. The driveway curved around the back of the houses that were on the road, 240 yards to our front door. AND - IT WAS 6 MILES AWAY FROM SKULLKRUSHERS WRESTLING SCHOOL!!!!

THERE'S A PLACE FOR US

Peace and tranquility at last. At last we were absolutely on our own. We both sighed a collective sigh of relief. But just as we thought we were all alone at last, down our driveway comes Bernard the Boy from Belgium - he was riding a bike he had borrowed from a neighbor.

"Adrian - could you show me that 'Chicken-wing' again?! - COULD I?!!!!!

GARY ALBRIGHT

Gary was a big boy - he stood 6 feet 3 inches and was definitely a 'Mighty Big Boy for his age.' He also weighed a very hefty 353 pounds. He invited Tony Charles, Linda and myself to his home in Pensacola, to watch him Wrestling on a pre-recorded TV pay-per-view from Japan. He would be wrestling against the Japanese wrestler, Toshiaki Kawada.

"Come early," he told us, "We're having a Barbeque, poolside." It was a lovely sunny day. The food was excellent, so was Gary's Japanese wrestling contest. We all watched it on the biggest screen TV that I had ever seen up to that time. After the wrestling had ended, we all went back to the Barbeque, to discuss the contest and eat some more. We were all thus engaged, when Gary's phone rang. It was Billy Robinson. Billy himself had just watched Gary's contest on TV, and had phoned Gary to talk about it. When Gary told Billy that I was there, Billy asked to speak to me. I hadn't seen Billy since before he had left Britain decades ago.

"How long have you been retired?" was one of the first questions Billy asked me.

"I haven't retired Billy," I told him, "I'm wrestling almost every night."

"Come on - you're joking right!" Billy argued, "You used to wrestle hard, like I did - I'll bet you're all fucked up - like I am!" he admitted.

"I am not fucked up, and I am still wrestling Billy." I told him. Billy seemed disappointed to learn that I was still very much in one piece, and still wrestling regularly.

"Ask Gary if I'm still wrestling." I suggested, and handed the phone back to Gary. Gary told me later that Billy still tried to teach wrestling, but was so badly crippled, from all those years of wear and tear, that his students had to lift him in and out of the ring. Then they had to help him get down onto the mat when he was teaching groundwork, then back up when he had finished.

Very sad, Billy was a fantastic wrestler in his time - a real credit to Billy Riley's 'Snake-pit.'

What was also very sad was that just 5 years later, January 7th, 2000, big Gary died. He was 36 years old.

BLOND SCALP versus BLACK WAR-BONNET

A pair of Attorneys from Tallahassee phoned me, and told me they wanted to be wrestling promoters. They also wanted to open their own wrestling school. Thirdly they wanted Linda and I to help them. Their promotion was to be called 'Universal Pro Wrestling'. They already had their own 'World Heavyweight Title Belt' and told me they were ready to promote a tournament, the winner of which would be crowned World champion. I was one of a dozen competitors. When the eliminations were over, the two finalists was Chief Black Eagle and myself. After being repeatedly tomahawk chopped and danced around, I easily outwrestled the Redskin to become The Universal World Heavyweight Wrestling Champion. Black Eagle immediately challenged me to a rematch. He also demanded an added stipulation. If I lost - which he promised I would, not only would I lose the World title, but I would also have my golden locks shaved off. I was more than happy to agree, as long as he agreed to my own stipulation. If I won, I would not only keep my title, but I would also take possession of his Black Feathered War-Bonnet. It turned out to be the best contest that I would ever take part in for that promotion - especially as I still have that Black War-Bonnet hanging on a wall in our Log-Cabin.

Very soon after Universal Wrestling Promotions went south. That was after the Attorneys and I straightened out a MASSIVE misunderstanding. For some strange reason, known only to themselves, the two Attorneys thought that they were going to get a half interest in 'Skullkrushers' Wrestling School. They even suggested, that it would be more convenient for them, if I relocated the school to Tallahassee. Where they got that very strange notion from is anyone's guess. I wasted no time in putting them straight, and that was the end of that. The whole venture was little more than a waste of time, but I still do have two very nice souvenirs - a beautiful Black War-Bonnet and a World Heavyweight Championship Wrestling Belt.

THE CASE OF THE MISSING KNEECAP

'Awesome' Al Savage began his training as a profession wrestler at Skullkrushers, soon after it first opened. He stood about 6 feet, weighed about 230 pounds. He had a good look about him, and I thought he showed a lot of potential. He was an avid disciple of 'The Macho Man' Randy Savage, hence the 'borrowed' surname. He also borrowed the look, and Linda and I created a whole wardrobe of 'Macho-Man' style jackets and tights for him to complete his image. He, like a number of my other students often became my opponents for various promoters that I wrestled for. He was a good heel, and we regularly had excellent contests against each other.

A number of years later 'The Awesome One,' began booking and matchmaking for some dope who wanted to be a wrestling promoter. The enterprise was short lived - but unfortunately for me, not short enough.

The promotion was fairly local, so I would send a number of my student wrestlers to his shows. I imagined that as they were fellow Skullkrushers, and he was the booker, he would possibly give them a start in the business. I was very disappointed - he even made them buy tickets to get in! I had told them that 'Awesome' Al was a nice guy - they told me that they thought he was a real jerk. Collectively, they told me that he treated all his wrestlers like crap. He tried to pose as some big superstar, by talking down to everyone. Deservedly attendance at their shows began dwindling. In order to bring it back up, they decided to bring in wrestlers who could put arses on seats. 'Bullet' Bob Armstrong and both Linda and I were invited to perform at one of their venues in Citronelle, Alabama - the show was packed. I would be wrestling against 'Awesome' Al. As I sat down and began lacing up my boots, Al brought his chair over and placed it in front of me, with its back facing mine.

"I'll tell you what I think we'll do in our match," he began to tell me. He went on to relate move for move, from the sound of the bell that heralded the start of our contest. I laughed, he knew I didn't do it that way, I thought he was joking. He turned out to be serious. His conception of what I taught had REALLY DETERIATED! I had taught him much better than that.

"We'll just go in there and wrestle," I told him, "is there anything fancy you would like to do before I beat you?" I inquired. There was - towards the end of the match, he would get some heel heat. While I was recovering and slowly climbing back to my feet after a slam, he would be climbing the ropes onto the corner post. The second I was standing erect, he would dive high into the air [Macho-man Savage like] and land across my chest, knocking me back down for a near pin fall. But, I would use the impetus to continue the motion, so that I would roll over and end up on top, where I would score the winning fall. The contest went well, I ad-libbed as I always did. At the finish, I got slammed, then watched through the corner of my eye, to ensure that he had got to the top of the corner post, by the time I had staggered back to my feet. Savage then leapt high into the air above me - BUT - THE SILLY BASTARD MISSED MY CHEST BY A MILE!!! He came down instead onto my legs - as I went down I felt my right knee SNAP!!! I didn't know what had happened, but I actually hoped that my right knee was only dislocated. But when I first examined it, I couldn't find my knee. When I did find it, it was more than dislocated. I found that the bottom of my kneecap was where the top of my kneecap should have been. With Linda's help I made it back to the dressing room.

'Awkward' Al Savage came running in and asked me what happened.

"You forgot the first thing I ever taught you," I told him, "if you don't know how to do something - don't do it."

"I'm sorry," he told me, "In a way, I would rather that it was me, who got injured instead of you."

"Yeah - that makes two of us!" I replied.

The promoter promised that his insurance would take care of all my medical bills - he lied. I did have my own insurance, but it still cost me many thousands of dollars out of my own pocket.

After surgery, when my kneecap was reattached to my shins, I had to undergo weeks of painful and exhausting rehab. Once again I was advised that my professional wrestling days were over. I was now in my late 50s, so it was obvious that my pro wrestling days were over - OBVIOUS TO WHO?!!!!!

If I don't like the advice I am given, then I won't heed it. But this time, it was more than my love of wrestling, or my natural stubbornness, that made me determined that this was not the end of my career. I remembered when I had wrestled for Roland Bock, during my first German tour. I could have liked Roland, but the one thing that marred that friendship was his continual boasting that it was he, who finished the wrestling career of the mighty George Gordienko. Roland was famous for his devastating suplex. It was with this maneuver that he hurled Gordienko right out of the ring. Big George hit the ring apron before landing on the arena floor. Gordienko had broken his leg. Big George Gordienko never wrestled again. I soon lost count of how many times I heard Roland Bock tell the story of his ultimate triumph.

If I called it quits now, 'Awesome' Al Savage would get the credit. He would go down in history as the man who ended my career. I DON'T THINK SO!!! Not if I had to crawl to the ring.

He almost did it, but - ALMOST doesn't count - if you're penniless and you ALMOST win a million dollars - the bottom line is, you're still penniless.

LESSONS

Obviously I taught wresting at Skullkrushers, I also taught wrestling psychology, but, I was quite amazed by how much I learned myself as a result. While explaining so many misconceptions that most people have about professional wrestling, often caused me to reassess what I knew myself. It made me look at so much I took for granted, from a different angle. For instance, I explained that in most counties, Wrestlers lead with their left hand when they initially come to grips. Each contestant grabs the other behind the neck with their left hand. Then with their right hand they grip the bend of the opponents left arm. What is known as 'collar and elbow. As I said, in most countries. In France everything was completely opposite, in Mexico, they would grab anything they could get hold of. In most countries it would then be much easier to apply a hold on the left arm, or the left leg, which was the way it was done - in most countries.

"I'm left-handed," one of my students told me, "So is it okay for me to come in with my right hand?"

"Only if you wrestle in France, or Mexico." I told him. But, then a thought struck me. It crossed my mind, that maybe, we could possibly develop a unique style for that particular student wrestler, if we could turn that hindrance into an asset. I can't say that it turned out to be a monumental success in practice, but it did give me cause to think outside the box somewhat.

Another thing that gave me food for thought, was when I first wrestled with a student who called himself 'Chains.' Chains stood about 6 feet 7 inches and weighed a little over 300 pounds. He had long black hair, a Goatee beard, a huge chest, broad shoulders and very large tattooed arms. His size was absolutely natural, he had never even lifted weights before he came to Skullkrushers. I remember envying his size and look. I had found it difficult at times, to be taken seriously, due to my own lack of size.

"We'll," I told him, "You must admit that in spite of my smaller stature, I did eventually make a big name for myself. Just imagine what I could have done if I'd been blessed with your size."

"If you had been as big as me - you may not have done nearly as well as you have." Chains replied. I thought he was being cheeky at first, and I'm sure my facial expression portrayed that very thought. So he quickly added,

"I'm not trying to be a smartass - what I mean is, that because of your size, you really worked hard. You had to do everything you could possibly do to make up for it - and it really worked for you. If you'd had my size, it would have been easier, and you wouldn't have needed to work so hard. You could have ended up, just being another big wrestler, instead of the unique Superstar you became."

DAMN - I COULDN'T ARGUE WITH THAT COULD I?!!!

Talking of BIG Guys and potential. We had a guy who stood 7 feet tall, weighed well in excess of 300 pounds, he had a shaven head, a black forked beard. He looked fantastic - Like a Giant Emperor Ming. He called himself 'Mr. Big', which I thought was bloody unimaginative, but worse than that, this modern day Goliath had all the confidence of a Field mouse in Kestrel country. He did wrestle for a while after leaving Skullkrushers, mostly for his own little promotion, but I have heard nothing of him after that. Then Swedish Kenneth Svennson, was about 6 feet 8 inches, weighing close to 300 pounds. Nicest guy one would wish to meet, but obsessed with his own failure, and how he could possibly deal with it. I did manage to talk enough backbone into him, so that after returning to Sweden he did wrestle for a while, but I never heard that he even got close to enjoying the kind of success he could have. Give me a little guy with GUTS any day of the week!

Amongst some of the smaller students, there are a few that stood out, and made much more of an impression, than the aforementioned extra BIG BOYS. Although, because of their lack of size, I wondered if these were cut out to be pro wrestlers in the States. But the fact that I myself had been initially written off, before and even during my career, the last thing I would do is piss on anyone else's dreams. Matt Maverick, Ken Banks, two smaller guys - both made it - both are still wrestling - AND when I say wrestling, I mean WRESTLING! A couple of Britishers, Paul Tyrell and Stu Allen, were both puny young kids when they first came to Skullkrushers. Paul is still a smaller wrestler, but a very skillful one, and a credit to our sport. Stu Allen may have been a tad over 6 feet tall when he first came to Skullkrushers, but was just a gangly young boy, whose neck was no thicker than my ankle. I'll be honest, I really didn't think he stood much of a chance. Not only did he prove me wrong, by becoming a great wrestler, he even turned into a huge MONSTER. He Wrestles as 'The Dominator' and his beautiful Wife 'Skarlett' 'The Bombshell from Hell' is a wrestler too and DAMN THAT GIRL CAN REALLY WRESTLE. As well as being a really impressive Lady Wrestler, Skarlett is also his Valet/manager.

Little Stu was like David Banner - now he is 'The Incredible Hulk.' He wrestled on a card in Britain, against another Monster from Skullkrushers, 'Mike the Python,' 6 feet 6 inches, 275 pounds of muscle. On the same card was another of my favorites from our school, Francisco Ciasco.

Bernard Van Dam from Belgium, was just a slim, but good looking young man when he first arrived. But right from the beginning, Bernard just oozed charisma. I always said if there was a crowd of a thousand wrestlers walking down the Road, Bernard would be the one you would notice - and the one you would remember. Bernard gained about 40 pounds of muscle and went on to win The European Wrestling Championship - a title that I have held myself on a number of occasions.

Stud Hammer, stood 6 feet 2 inches, had a 64 inch chest and his neck measured as much as my thigh. He was one of the strongest men I have ever met. Aaron Arsenal was another talented monster. Icelander, Dolph the Slayer, Australian, Jack Thunder and from the States, Jason Ultimo, Colt Steel and Tommy Johnson, all great guys.

We had Keith Wong from The Cayman Islands, he wanted to call himself 'The Caribbean Pirate.' Very soon all the other students were calling him 'The Caribbean Primate,' but then that's wrestlers for you. Keith worshiped me - BUT - he would do everything he could NOT to get into the ring with me. He would wrestle - or at least perform his own version of wrestling, with any of the other students, but if I attempted to show him anything, he employed every excuse under the Sun to avoid it. His favorite excuse, was also a favorite with all the other students,

"Oh, Mon - I'm real hungry, Mon, let's go to Barnhills."

Barnhills was a Buffet Restaurant, just a few hundred yards away from Skullkrushers. Keith would treat Linda and I, and every student, to an all you could eat meal just to avoid getting one single wrestling lesson from me. Of course, after we had eaten, Keith would be too full to wrestle and would have to sleep. But he did have connections all over The Caribbean, and he set up a wrestling tour of all the major Caribbean Islands. He really pulled out all of the stops to get me to be a part of the tour, but I had new students coming to the school all the time. But he took a full wrestling card from the school. He claimed that he would never employ a wrestler on any of his tours, unless that wrestler had been trained by 'Exotic' Adrian Street. It probably didn't cross his mind, that that would exclude him from his own tour. But amongst the wrestlers who did take the tour was 'Awesome' Al Savage and Stu Allen. Some of the tales I heard later when my wrestlers returned to Skullkrushers were hilarious - but I will Let Stu relate those stories when he writes his own autobiography.

When I reached the age of 60, I was congratulated by my students, who all thought I was wearing very well,

"Damn," they told me, "I hope I will look as good as you do when I reach 60 years old!"

"Well," I replied, "You'd better start lifting those weights, because you don't look as good as I do now."

"No - seriously," they continued, "Now that you're at the twilight of your career, you must be really proud to be teaching so many future champions."

"Sometimes I am proud," I admitted, "but as often as not, I feel more like a fucking Babysitter, than a trainer of Champions." They all laughed, not really appreciating how serious I was.

As every wrestling fan knows, Mick Foley was most famous for performing all kinds of death defying feats, like getting slammed off the top of sky high cages, and crashing through tables on his journey back to terrafirma. He also fought on mountains of thumbtacks, glass and rejoiced when the ring ropes were replaced with razor-wire. The result of this style of 'wrestling' spelled many painful injuries for this Dare anything Daredevil. Not wanting him to continue in this direction, Vince McMahon suggested that Mick attended Skullkrushers, and actually learn to wrestle. I had wrestled against Mick for promoter, Ben Masters, in Georgia. I had also wrestled him when he was 'Cactus Jack' for Continental. Linda and I also created the costume for his 'Dude Love' character, so we were well acquainted. I have to say that underneath that tough as nails exterior, was one of the nicest people I have met - inside or outside the World of wrestling. He bought a home for himself and his family, about 20 miles away from Skullkrushers. Then he opened a Gym for weightlifting, bodybuilding and fitness. He invited Linda and I to train there free of charge. He also gave me a special deal on fees for any of my Skullkrusher's students if they wanted to work-out there. I would buy my students their first months fee. As you can imagine, my students were absolutely thrilled that Mick Foley was a fellow student during that period.

Rico Costantino had been an 'American Gladiator Champion' before he began wrestling for the WWE. He had been trained to wrestle initially by Jesse Hernandez, who along with Bill Anderson, I regarded as amongst the best trainers. It was Vince McMahon himself, who ordered Rico to come to Skullkrushers, in order to learn how to perform the 'EXOTIC' gimmick, from the most Exotic wrestler to ever set foot in a wrestling ring. In the limited time we had, I only taught Rico a few wrestling moves in order to enhance his image. What I concentrated more on, was attitude and psychology. Rico was an intelligent guy, he latched on very quickly to what I told him. I really looked forward to seeing how well my input would go over. I watched the new Rico make his TV debut.

To say I was very disappointed with the result, was - all I can say is GGGGGGRRRRRR!!!!

The new Rico enters the ring like 'Exotic' Adrian Street - he has a sexy Lady Valet - just like 'Exotic' Adrian Street. So far - so good. Then it all goes SOUTH!!! He then plays the 'straight-man' - pun intended - to his glamorous Valet, who was played by Miss Jackie. That was the wrong way around. Jackie posed seductively, crawled between Rico's legs, slid up his body and embraced him like a Queen would do to her pet sex slave. If Linda had ever done anything like that, I would have had no choice but to SWAT her like a fly. When I was a villain, as Rico was now supposed to be, I got much of my heat by treating Linda like an unappreciated slave. I would even make her drop onto her hands and knees ringside, so that I could enter the ring by stepping on her back.

I don't blame Rico - you shouldn't either. Blame Vince McMahon's stupid, ignorant scriptwriters, who probably had such a hard-on for Miss Jackie, that they gave her the dominant role. If they wanted to make my gimmick work for Rico, then Rico would be the bright shining Star. Miss Jackie would be no more than a complimentary satellite, whose duty it would be to make her Lord and Master shine ever brighter. But, what would one expect, from a promotion that knows absolutely NOTHING about wrestling.

Whenever his Lordship, Steven Regal was wrestling in Pensacola, he would often come by. Sometimes he would stay with us. On such occasions, he would visit Skullkrushers, and much to the delight of my students, would give them a demonstration of good old fashion 'British style wrestling.' It was Steve who introduced us to Triple H, who invited Linda and I to a meal with him and Steve Regal. What excellent company to share a Steak with. Earlier that evening we were invited backstage at the WWE show, where we met up again with another old friend, Big Mark 'The Undertaker.' We also met Vince McMahon for the first time, when he suddenly leapt into a photo we were taking of Linda and I with Mark and 'The Big Show'.

SO LITTLE TIME - SO MANY PEOPLE TO PISS OFF!

My oldest Son Adrian had been staying with us, and we were enjoying his stay as much as we hoped he was. We had taken a trip up to Tupelo and visited Elvis' Birth place. We had been delighted with the liberties we had been allowed to take by the managers, all who had been great fans of ours, when Linda and I had wrestled in Tupelo over the years. They took photos of us lounging on the very bed that 'The King' had been born in, and just about everywhere else in the house. Adrian was in his element signing autographs for the managers and other visitors, while sitting in Elvis' favorite chair.

We also enjoyed 'Walking in Memphis' when we visited 'Gracelands' and Beal Street. It now seems like an omen. In Beal Street we took a photo of Adrian standing in front of a poster bearing the image of Buddy Holly - who Adrian seemed to resemble. A few of years later, Adrian auditioned for a 'Musical Stage Play' entitled 'Buddy.' Adrian got the title role and played the Legendary Buddy Holly. I had always been a great fan, my son had been bombarded with 'Rock 'n' Roll' from the time he was born. Especially Elvis and Buddy.

Adrian returned to Britain, but soon after came back, to find that in the meantime, my Sister Pam and Brother-in-law Mike had come to us for a visit. Once again Adrian returned to Britain while Pam and Mike was still with us. Just before Pam and Mike returned to Britain, I began experiencing a mild discomfort in my throat. It was about that time that I began spitting blood. At first I wasn't overly concerned, but soon I was coughing up great gobs of the stuff, and realized I needed to seek a little medical advice.

My first visit to the Hospital resulted in them cauterizing the back of my throat and then advising me to return to the Hospital if the bleeding reoccurred. Well, it did reoccur. Next morning I began to cough, and blood poured out of my mouth and back down my throat. I returned to the Hospital, they repeated the treatment, but later that day I had to go back and get it all done again. It was not long before I was visiting the Hospital every morning.

While Linda drove, I would sit in the passenger seat with a plastic bucket on my lap to catch the blood as I coughed and retched into it. Often the bottom of the bucket would be swimming before we arrived at the Hospital - then all that happened was cauterization - go home - cough - bleed - return to Hospital. Eventually they sent me to see a 'Specialist' in Pensacola. He looked, poked and cauterized. After leaving his office we never even made it to our car before the blood poured again. We turned back around, walked back to the 'Specialist's' office and he cauterized my throat once more.

Next morning, I awoke, coughed and blood came out like thick congealed ropes. When we started out for the car, Linda handed me the plastic bucket. I handed it back - instead I took a large roll of kitchen paper. On our way to the Hospital, I just allowed the blood to pour into the heap of paper on my lap. By the time we arrived the paper was just one big, Bloody red, dripping mass. It was absolutely saturated. I took it with me into the Hospital.

The looks of horror I received from everyone as I marched into casualty almost made me laugh - BOY - do I know how to make a grand entrance!

I didn't laugh - instead I coughed, and more blood poured into the soggy mass I was holding against my chest. Nurses rushed to my aid. I had never received such prompt attention. I was ushered into an examination room, where one of the suggestions was to cauterize my bleeding throat! Another Doctor thought it might be more serious and I was kept in overnight and told that I would be given a biopsy by a Dr. Lurton the next morning.

I was released and told to visit Dr. Lurton's office in a couple of days in order to get the lab results. I did, and this is what Dr. Lurton told me,

"Mr. Street, I'm sorry to tell you, that you have a very malignant type of throat cancer. I'm going to give it to you straight. You are not going to make it out of this - I suggest you go home and put your affairs in order."

"I'm not going to die yet, Doctor," I replied, "there's still too many people in the World I haven't pissed of yet!"

I would have to receive radiation and chemotherapy treatment and was advised to gain as much weight as I could. They told me, that during my treatment I would lose my appetite, and it would probably help if I added a bit of extra bulk in anticipation. I was down from over 200 pounds and was hovering around about 185 pounds at that time. I have never had any trouble gaining or losing weight, so taking the advice I had been given, I quickly bulked up to about 205 pounds. That did not last long - thanks to the chemo.

As soon as the effects of radiation and chemo kicked in my appetite disappeared and was replaced by chronic nausea. I didn't want to eat anything. A favorite dish, like a juicy, rare Fillet-Mignon was less appealing than a plate full of hot Dog shit - and smelled twice as bad. I couldn't drink anything but a small sip of water, and even that made me feel ill.

I had a tube inserted into the inside of my arm, that was threaded up into my chest. It ached like Hell, all the time, but was necessary to help feed, hydrate me and administer medicine, including chemo. They made a special mask that was used to screw my head into a fixed position on the table that I lay for my radiation sessions. It was marked in the areas where the radiation was to be directed, in order to try to protect as much of the surrounding tissue as possible. The medicine they gave me before I took the radiation made me sick, and in spite of the care that was taken to protect anything but the cancer cells, my saliva glands and carotid arteries were permanently damaged. So were my upper back teeth which I eventually had replaced with implants.

Most often after that treatment was completed for the day, I would throw up in the nearest rest room. It's a rough exercise, throwing up on an empty stomach.

It seemed all I could keep down at home was a couple of spoonfuls of noodles washed down with a few sips of Beef Broth. My weight dropped dramatically, from 205 pounds down to about 150 pounds. All the hair on my head and body came out in clumps. I grabbed a razor, and finished the job that the chemo had began. The only hair I had left was my eyebrows and eyelashes.

I was told that the most probable cause of my illness was the secondhand tobacco smoke, that I had been subjected to. In smoke filled arenas, dressing rooms and various vehicles, for hours on end, while traveling to and from various venues over the decades.

I stayed in Hospital for the first couple of weeks of my treatment. Linda was given a recliner to sit in beside my bed, and she stayed with me, night and day, all the while I was in there. In spite of my condition, and the fact that I would be permanently connected to an IV Pole, I would get out of bed and MOVE. I would stride around the corridors as fast as I could go, while Linda trotted behind me, pushing the IV Pole that I was attached to. I would walk up as many steps on the stairs as the length of the IV tubes would allow, and perform a set of pushups at the top and another back at the bottom. We would walk a few times a day to where the newborn Babies would be lined up behind glass windows, in rows of incubators. I would then pester the nurses, pretending that I wanted to feed peanuts to the little Babies. Gotta laugh, even when you really don't feel like it.

Although I really appreciated Linda being with me 24 hours a day, while in hospital, meal times were a problem. Both Linda and I would be served the same meals - Linda always enjoyed hers. I couldn't stand the smell of food, let alone eat it. I would make Linda eat her food in the furthest corner of the room, and still the smell of it made me feel as sick as a Parrot.

I just had to get out of the hospital, and the dreadful smell of food. I did get out, but I would have to return for my treatment 5 days a week. I would arrive there early morning and get hitched up to the IV pole, that fed me, and administered the chemo and various medicines/nutrients to keep me going. This went on for weeks.

I remember sitting alone in our garden. I looked at the Trees, Flowers, Birds, Butterflies, the Sky, the Clouds, and thinking,

'If I do die, I'm really going to miss all this.' I really couldn't imagine that this was at last the end. So once again, I decided not to listen to people's advice, who thought they knew best. I decided to do it the only way I knew how - MY WAY!

In spite of being constantly sick, I would stop at Gulf Breeze, Fitness Gym on the way back home from the Hospital. By now I was so weak, I could barely keep up with the poundage that Linda used when lifting weights. My stamina too, was almost nonexistent. Ten to fifteen minutes was enough to exhaust me. I would go home and sleep until it was time to go to bed. Then get up next morning and do it all again.

When my treatment was finally complete, the radiation Nurses gave me a diploma that they had all signed. They told me that I was the toughest person they had ever treated.

"We threw the kitchen sink at you," they told me, "we had bets between us, that you would never be able to complete your treatment - at least not without taking breaks to help you recover." They really were a great bunch of Ladies.

I remember proudly clutching my diploma, as Linda and I walked back into the waiting room. We found everyone there standing up staring at a TV, that was set up in the corner of the room.. There was a picture of the Twin-Towers, as an aircraft flew right into it. We thought it was a movie.

"NO - NO IT'S REAL!!!" We were told. We blinked and looked again, and another aircraft flew right into the other tower. Now we knew it wasn't real. I expected to see Bruce Wills, Sylvester Stallone, or Arnold. But the distress displayed by all the other patients in the room belied that scenario.

It was real - now I felt sick in the stomach, for an entirely different reason.

****

Although we had medical insurance, it certainly didn't cover everything. We had not been able to work, or wrestle, so we had earned nothing for months. Meanwhile expenses just kept piling up. Then the tax man hit us like a mad tornado. Financially we were all but wiped out.

The taxman was relentless and ruthlessly unsympathetic, when I explained our situation. While I was attempting to negotiate a deal, unbeknown to me, the interest on my tax debt kept mounting up. I was suddenly made aware that we now owed thousands of dollars more than we had originally owed. I told the taxman truthfully that we just didn't have the money.

"Sell your rental property and use that to pay your tax." he told me.

"That is all the money we have coming in, right now," I explained, "if we sell that, we have nothing."

"Sell your rental properties - pay your tax - then get yourself a menial job." he suggested.

You can never imagine how many times I have fantasized the pleasure I would have derived out of discussing my tax problems, face to face with the taxman - in a secret soundproof room, somewhere that no one else in the World knew about. Oh well - we all have dreams!

We managed to secure a loan from our bank to satisfy the tax, and began working very hard in order to make a physical and financial comeback.

I do not like paying interest on anything, so it's very fortunate that I had already paid off the mortgages on both the apartments and our home. Although, that too had helped deplete the coffers.

Nevertheless we were not out of the woods yet. I was still having to take monthly checkups with three different Doctors. Dr. 'Mr. Cheerful' Lurton told me, I was still ten times more likely to contract the disease again, than any other person was likely to get it in the first place.

All the time I had been receiving that awful treatment, in spite of feeling terrible, from both the medicine and the lack of nourishment, I had continued going to the gym and lifting weights. All through that period I had become weaker and weaker, but I refused to give up. Just two weeks after I finished my treatment, and my appetite had began to return. My strength also returned, and I was soon using the same heavy weights I had enjoyed lifting before I had become ill.

My hair grew back, but it was not the same as it used to be. My hair is naturally straight, now it was coarse and curly. I didn't like it. If I can't have things the way I want them, then I don't want them at all - I got my razor back out.

It was surmised by just about everyone, that my already lengthy wrestling career was at an end. Well we all know how that one goes. I won't allow anyone, or anything to dictate what I can and cannot do. I was training hard with a return to wrestling in mind.

This is a newspaper article written by my good friend and wrestling Superstar 'Bullet' Bob Armstrong.

ADRIAN STREET - BACK AND LOOKING BETTER THAN EVER

Adrian Street, A.K.A. 'THE EXOTIC ONE,' is a tough customer, not only in the ring but in character as well. Less than a couple of years ago Adrian had a severe bout of throat cancer. His weight dropped dramatically. His hair fell out from the cancer treatment, and food tasted horrible to him.

During this terrible time, he continued to train as much as he could. It took almost one year, but THE EXOTIC ONE beat cancer and is back looking better than ever. He is in his early sixties now but looks twenty years younger. I had the pleasure of watching him give his young opponent a REAL wrestling lesson two weeks ago. He won the match in ten minutes and could have won in two.

The EXOTIC ADRIAN STREET is back in full force and is always with his lovely valet, 'MISS LINDA.' This pair always treat the crowd by wearing ring attire a Las Vegas show would be proud of. Adrian makes his own outfits for the ring as well as all of Bullet Bob's wrestling gear. I'm happy to call them both friends. - Bullet Bob Armstrong.

It was then that I really began to realize that Linda's loyalty and devotion during that awful period, deserved a lot more than what she would have been left with if Dr. Lurton's prediction had borne fruit. I knew I needed to help protect her from any predicament that a reoccurrence of my illness, or any other disaster that might befall us. But, we were so busy, just trying to catch up, that time just slipped through my fingers. When I wasn't wrestling myself, I was teaching wrestling and designing costumes for other wrestlers.

CHLOE & TAYLOR

My Daughter Amanda came out for a visit in 2002. With her was her husband John and my two Grandchildren, 9 year old Chloe, and her Brother, 5 year old Taylor. The last time I had seen Chloe was when I was in Britain on my way back to the States from Japan. Then Chloe was just a little baby about 14 months old. She had really grown into a very beautiful young Girl. Must take after me. Little Taylor was my Birthday buddy. He had been born on my 58th Birthday, December the 5th. As this was just coming up to Amanda's Birthday, I sent them all airline tickets and planned a special holiday treat for them all. Linda and I took them to Orlando and stayed at a resort in The Disney Complex. We all had a great holiday. They have visited since in 2007 and in 2009.

HURRICANE IVAN

No 'Hurricane Ivan' was not a professional wrestler - it was just a Hurricane.

The first time we were aware of a Hurricane in our neck of the woods, was soon after we moved into one of our own apartments. Ken Wayne and Danny Davis were tenants of another one. It was they who warned us that there was a Hurricane heading in our direction, and they told us that as a result, they were both heading for higher ground. I was inclined to stay put and ride out the storm. My motive for wanting to stay was out of curiosity as much as anything else. I had never experienced a Hurricane and I wondered what they were like. As Ken and Danny were loading some of their valuables into their cars, the weather really began to deteriorate. Linda was becoming a little nervous, as we could now hear the storm begin roaring in the Gulf. We decided then to follow Ken and Danny out of Dodge. We all ended up well inland, in a hotel in Alabama, close to the Georgia border.

The next bad storm I remember was Hurricane Erin, August 3rd 1995. We were living in our log cabin by then, and that time we decided to stay and sit it out.

Now that turned out to be an experience. Damn - if I had clicked my Ruby Slippers together, I think we would have ended up in Kansas instead of the Gulf Coast. The wind and rain was tremendous!!! We never, ever imagined it could be so powerful. The only room in our cabin without windows is our downstairs bathroom, so we dragged a King-sized mattress out of one of the bedrooms into that bathroom. We dove onto the mattress and slammed the door shut. The wind howled like a constipated banshee, so very loud we couldn't hear ourselves think. I can't remember how long that lasted before it gradually became increasingly silent. We left the bathroom and crept outside onto our front porch. The sky was a milky hue, it almost looked as though the sun wanted to shine. It was so very quiet, hardly a breeze, we were now dead centre of the storm, it felt as though we were the only two people left on Earth. But gradually the wind once again began to increase. We noticed that when the storm had began the wind had been blowing from our left to our right, now as the eye of Erin began to pass by, the wind grew in strength, but it was blowing in the opposite direction. We sat and watched as the storm once again gathered strength. Trees cracked, broke, fell. Huge branches were torn off the trunks and flying through the air like carpets from the 'Arabian Nights'. Some trees were torn right out of the ground by their roots. We had a huge Pine tree that had the bark blown of it before it twisted right around, and then came crashing down, right across our driveway. We quickly popped back indoors and into our cozy, but noisy sanctuary.

At last Erin charged north, leaving nothing but shattered devastation in its wake. We have an almost two acre garden, that was now like nothing we had ever seen before in real life. I figured there was good news and bad news. The bad news was that we had tons of huge broken branches and felled trees in gigantic heaps, tangled all over our garden. The good news is that we have a wood burning stove.

Chainsaw time.

Well Linda and I worked and worked and worked. Sawing, carrying, dragging, untangling and stacking ton after ton of wood. Then trying to straighten and tidy up everything that the giant storm had hurled into disarray. We were just beginning to see a faint glimmer of light at the end of the tunnel, our garden was just beginning to look beautiful again when - HERE WE GO AGAIN!!!! Just a couple of months later October 4th, we got another direct hit - Hurricane Opal was coming to town.

This time we decided that discretion was indeed the better part of valor. We would not remain to welcome Opal - instead we would piss off as quickly as we could. That turned out to be better said than done. We had decided to flee to Birmingham, Alabama, although our journey could hardly be described as fleeing. We crawled for the whole 260 mile trip in a traffic jam from Hell. Everyone planned to fight another day. It must have taken us half a day. Trying to find somewhere to stay did not help the cause, everywhere was filled with Opal's refugees. At last we found a hotel in Birmingham. We had brought food and wine with us from home, so we settled down in our room to watch Opal's progress on TV. We didn't get to watch it for long, as the storm had caught up with us. All the power in our hotel was knocked completely out. We sat there in the dark completely ignorant of anything that Opal had done, or was going to do. We went to sleep serenaded by the very powerful wind rattling our windows.

Next morning we phoned our friend, Linda Marx. We went to her house to find out what we could about Opal and what damage it had caused. Before we left on our return journey home, Linda Marx made us promise that if we ever had another Hurricane threatening our wellbeing that we would go and stay with her. We were very happy and grateful to agree.

Getting back home was another nightmare. The closer we got to home the more gas stations were closed, the few that were not closed, had a lineup of vehicles miles long. When we finally reached the outskirts of our own territory, evidence of the storm became more and more pronounced. When we finally reached our own driveway, we were absolutely appalled at the sight that awaited us. From our mail box to our front door is over 240 yards - now it was over 240 yards of a heaped mountain of tangled lumber. We left our van on the road, and had to climb over and under broken limbs and trunks from the road right up to our front door. It took days of hard work just to clear enough of the debris off the pathway to bring our van in off the road. We took our time clearing the remainder of our garden, two storms in such a short space of time really dampened our enthusiasm for gardening.

After Opal we got a nine year reprieve. Then in September 2004 we got IVAN!!! We knew it was going to be bad, so when it looked certain to be coming our way, we packed up and went to stay with Linda Marx in Birmingham. Linda M. knew we would want to follow Ivan's progress, so she went out and bought a 47 inch TV for the bedroom that Linda and I would be sleeping in while we stayed with her. Didn't I tell you Linda Marx has class?!

When we returned home in the aftermath of Ivan, we were greeted by the same kind of devastation that had become too familiar. After assessing the damage around our home, we went to do likewise to our rental apartments and wrestling school. The apartment building needed an entire new roof. The school buildings came off even worse. As well as the original building, I had eventually removed the swimming pool in order to make room for another building that contained a professional wrestling ring. Ivan had caused the original building to spring many leaks. The new building was MISSING! When I say missing - I'm saying there was no trace that it had ever existed. We're talking 'Twilight Zone'. The professional wrestling ring was just sitting there all on its own. The building the ring had been in, had gone with Ivan.

I decided then that I would close Skullkrushers Wrestling School, and officially that was that. But I did make a few exceptions and taught a few more student wrestlers. Tony Scarlo brought over a team of wrestlers that he had been training. That was a lot of fun, and Tony does know what he's talking about when it comes to WRESTLING. But their lessons were conducted, either in the wreckage of the original building, or in the ring outside. The ring outside sat there in all weathers, until I eventually sold it to a promoter.

Tony Charles, my good friend and my very first regular tag-team partner in 'The Welsh Wizards,' back in my British wrestling days. He now lived on the beach with his Wife, Pam. Or at least they did until Hurricane Ivan. All that was now left of their home was a sand dune. Either their home was crushed and buried - or maybe gone wherever Skullkrushers wrestling school had gone. The very fact that Skullkrushers was no more, left my rental apartments temporarily vacant, so I was able to give Tony and Pam a place to live, while their home was being rebuilt on the same site where their old home had been.

Back at the Log Cabin we had lots of work to do, especially all over our garden. Once again there were downed trees and torn branches everywhere. A giant Pine tree had fallen and crushed the top of our greenhouse. The base was still partially rooted in the ground, while the first third of its length was on top of the greenhouse and the remainder loomed at an angle over a concrete patio and then over the driveway. I found that my 16 foot ladder would just reach the tree at about two thirds along its height, and I planned to cut it down in large sections. I started up my chainsaw, which I then held in my right hand as I ascended the ladder. I had to force my way through bushes and branches before I finally stood almost tippy-toe on the ladder's summit. I leaned over the tree as best I could and began sawing. Just one cut would reduce the giant Pine by one third its length. It was a bit of a struggle leaning sideway with the saw in one hand, but it seemed to be working. Deeper and deeper bit the saw, until with a great creak and groan the top third of the tree fell away. BUT - with all that weight suddenly gone, the rest of the tree shot up about six more feet into the air. I was thrown up and backwards about 20 feet into the air with a live chainsaw in my right hand and a concrete patio below me. I had the presence of mind to throw the chainsaw away from me and hoped that I wouldn't land on it. Whatever - I still had a long way to fall, The good news was, that there was a lot of displaced bushes between me and the concrete patio. The bad news was - they were very thorny Rose bushes. I didn't break my back or fracture my skull, but when I crawled out of the Roses I must have looked as though I had been trying to shag a Werewolf in a phone box.

Walking around our neighborhood was an experience in itself. You cannot imagine the devastation unless you saw it firsthand. I can only liken it to the sight I remembered when I visited my Grandmother in Bristol after the War in 1945. I'm not talking about the sight of my Grandmother - I'm talking about Bristol. Dust and rubble from horizon to horizon.

Just around the corner from where we lived looked like an endless trash heap. We walked up to a pier that protruded out into the sound. I walked on that pier almost every day after we had finished lifting weights. It was completely GONE!

Even though we share property boundaries with about a half dozen neighbors, they can't see us, and we can't see them. We have Trees, Bamboos, tall shrubs, all around us, and it's almost like living in our own private little valley. But when he heard my chainsaw roaring away, my next door neighbor Robert Heighton, fired up his own chainsaw and came to join me. Robert was a dab hand with a chainsaw, and between us the chaos began to transform itself into neat piles of logs, ready for Winter. I took a couple of photos of Robert hard at work to remind myself what a great neighbor he was. Little did I suspect that they would be the last photos ever taken of him.

Robert was a Firefighter and Paramedic. Answering an emergency call for a critical ill cardiac patient he flew in a helicopter ambulance to the rescue. Robert was amongst the three killed when the helicopter crashed. He was just 45 years old.

I had the two photos I had taken of Robert enlarged and framed, and gave them to Robert's Wife and two little Daughters. Such a shame, a lovely man, a lovely family.

The next year, July 2005, we saw the arrival of Hurricane Dennis. We took to the hills and went to stay with Linda Marx. On our return we found the same devastation all over again. We had barely finished clearing up from Ivan - now it was time to begin all over again. It was good that we had decided not to ride out the storm, as we found that almost one half of our roof had been blown away. What was left was hanging down, and looked like the lid of an opened Sardine can. I won't describe our efforts to clear everything up once again - I think you might well have the picture. But we do now have a metal roof which we hope will fare better in the future.

LORD ALFRED HAYES

I had known Al since the late 1950s when he wrestled as 'Judo' Al Hayes. Al was a trip, and talking about trips, if you were lucky enough to have him with you when you were traveling to a venue, even Dale Martin's horrible transport became bearable. Tales from Al just melted away the miles. Talking of tales, the last time I remember being in his company, was when we fought each other in the opening scenes of the movie 'Canterbury Tales'. In that fight, I won and received a Goat as my prize. A Goat may have been a strange payment, but it was a lot better than most the payments you would receive from Dale Martin in those days.

Al left Britain for the States before I did, at 6 feet 1 inch and weighing about 240 he had an advantage that I could never attain. But, we both did well. In all the years that we both wrestled in the U.S.A. our paths unfortunately never, ever crossed. The first opportunity to talk to him was even more unfortunate - when I learned that he was really very ill. I did know that he had been confined to a wheelchair for some time, as a result of so many years of occupational wear and tear, but I learned that his condition was now very serious. I wanted to tell him just how much he had inspired so many British wrestlers, myself included, and that his influence had really helped elevate the 'Golden Age' of British Wrestling.

I phoned him, and a Lady's voice answered the phone. I told her who I was and that I would like to talk to Al,

"Hello - who is this?" he asked. His voice was unmistakable - just like the times we'd traveled together decades earlier.

"This is Adrian - Adrian Street," I told him, "How are you?"

"Oh, thank you very much for calling - goodbye!" he replied, and put the phone down. I am certain that he didn't have a clue who I was. The date of my call was July 20th 2005. I was the last wrestler to ever speak to Lord Alfred Hayes. The very next day 21st of July 2005 Alfie died.

TAMPA WRESTLE REUNION 2005

I had never met 'Rowdy' Roddy Piper before Tampa Wrestle Reunion. We both marveled how many years we had both wrestled in the same areas, without our paths ever crossing before. Roddy was a great guy, funny and smart. So sad he is no longer with us. Other wrestlers who were at the reunion and are no longer with us include, Sherri Martelle, Dusty Rhodes, and Tommy Rogers.

There was also a few other wrestlers who I met there for the first time, 'Diamond' Dallas Page, Jimmy Snuka and one of my all time favorites, Bruno Sammartino. Bruno and I had a good long chat, a very impressive man.

There was a long list of great wrestling Legends who would be wrestling over a couple of days, to list them all would require that I write another book. I would be wrestling in the Battle Royal.

The Battle Royal was for the IWA Heavyweight Championship. Contestants included Greg Valentine, Norman Smiley, Bob Armstrong, Scott Armstrong, Brad Armstrong, Ronnie Garvin, Jake 'The Snake' Roberts, Shane Douglas, Virgil, Thunderfoot #1, Thunderfoot#2, Hack Meyers, Samu, Chavo Guerrero, The Warlord, Bugsy McGraw and myself. But, before the contest Chavo Guerrero approached me with a special request.

"You've wrestled in Mexico haven't you?" he began,

"Yes I have." I confirmed.

"Good - then you can do all the Lucha Libre high flying style," he stated, "I've asked if you and I could be taken out of the Battle Royal, and we can do a single match - Lucha Libre style."

You would have to go a very long way, to find anyone who disliked the Lucha-Libre style of wrestling more than I did. So I replied,

"I don't mind wrestling you in a single match - BUT - it will be wrestling - not that silly Mexican crap. It will also be a contest that I win and you lose - unless of course you can do anything to prevent that from happening."

Chavo had already spoken to Tom Pritchard, who was one of the reunion's matchmakers, and it was Tom who had given Chavo the okay for a single Lucha Libre style contest against me. After I had initially given Chavo my thoughts on the subject, he went off and brought back Tom Pritchard. Tom tried to talk me into complying with Chavo's wishes. I told Pritchard exactly what I had already told Chavo. I would be happy to wrestle him in a single contest - but it would not be Lucha Libre - it would be WRESTLING and Chavo would LOSE!

They decided to leave us both in the Battle Royal.

So the Battle Royal it was. I was amongst the last three to be eliminated, I was thrown over the top rope by Greg Valentine, who won the contest and became the new IWA Heavyweight Champion.

FAIRY TALE

Ever since Linda had nursed me back to super health, after my life threatening illness, I had my mind set on making her life more secure - just in case of a reoccurrence. It was March 2005 before I got a perfect opportunity to 'put my affairs in order.'

When Linda and I attended the annual get-together at 'The Gulf-Coast Wrestler's Reunion,' I had a very thrilling surprise waiting there for me.

Karl Lauer was there, and announced that I was to be made an 'Honoree' of the World famous Wrestler's Reunion, 'The Cauliflower Alley Club.'

Karl had been one of the first two wrestling promoters I had wrestled for in America. He was also a main wheel in the renowned Boxer and Wrestler reunion. The Club had been founded by wrestler/movie actor, Mike Mazurki. Only Boxers, Wrestlers, or Movie Stars who had played either Boxers, or Wrestlers could be elected as Honorees of the Club. Not only would I share that honor with the greats in Boxing and Wrestling, but also with great Stars, like James Cagney, Kirk Douglas, Jack Palance and Sylvester Stallone.

Karl Lauer's invitation to attend The Cauliflower Alley Club to receive my 'WALL OF FAME HONOREE AWARD,' refreshed a long overdue idea, that I had wanted to act on since I had still been sick in hospital. I phoned Karl and ran my thoughts by him. Would it be possible to contact a Priest, who could Marry Linda and I at The Cauliflower Alley Club's Banquet, when I received my award?

"We can go one better than that," Karl assured me, "one of our members, Jason Sanderson is an ordained Catholic Priest - he's a great Guy, and he can tell you how to go about it." Karl gave me Father Sanderson's phone number, I called him, then between Karl, Father Jason and myself we began putting our plan together, that we hoped would be a pleasant surprise for Linda.

There were a couple of downsides attached to keeping our plan a secret, and that was that there were many friends and family, who I would have liked to invite. But, with friends and family like I have, I was certain that it would end up being anything but a secret and a surprise for Linda. I knew that the more people who knew of our plan, the more likely that the Cat would be let out of the bag. So schtum was the word.

I was told that there was a record number of attendees that year, almost 600. Also that there had never before been so many professional wrestlers, under one roof at one time. They included Don Leo Jonathan, Killer Kowalski, Jack & Jerry Brisco, Bob Orton Sr., Danny Hodge, The Destroyer, Nick Bockwinkle, Ox Baker, Leo Garibaldi, Terry Funk, Bobby Heenan, Mad Dog & Butcher Vashon, Penny Banner, Jesse Hernandez, Harley Race, John Tolos, Red Bastien, Jack Armstrong, Larry Henning, Cheerleader Melisa, Paul Diamond, Pat Patterson, Brian Blair, Percy Pringle - [Paul Bearer] Mondo Guerrero, Manny Fernandez and many more.

It wasn't until the very day before the Banquet that I met 'The Mormon Giant,' Don Leo Jonathan for the first time in my life. I told him that he had been my Hero from the time I had been about 12 years old. I had been so inspired by him, that for the first four years of my wrestling career, I had wrestled under the name of Kid 'Tarzan' Jonathan. I also told him that I planned to propose to Linda that very night. To my delight he agreed to be my Best-Man the next evening, if Linda accepted my proposal.

That evening there was a Buffet, where presentations would be carried out and speeches made. I hardly tasted my food, as I waited in anticipation for the presentations.

I was called up onto the stage where I was presented with the ultimate prize of recognition by my peers. I was so choked up with emotion, I was hardly able to speak. But even though it was difficult, I explained just how honored I felt. Not only to be made a 'Wall of Fame Honoree.' but to be presented with it in the presence of so many of my childhood Heroes and Villains. Not only had they inspired me, but they had given my life a direction. They gave me a reason to live, made me who I was.

"I would say, it doesn't get any better than this," I told them, as I called Linda up onto the podium to stand beside me, "But, there is one thing that could make this better still - and that is, if Linda - the love of my life, agrees to marry me." I don't know if it sounded exactly like that, because by then I was crying like a Baby.

Thank goodness Linda said "YES."

Next day was very busy for Linda and I. Father Sanderson told us where to go to apply for a marriage license, and there was wedding rings to shop for.

The ceremony was to take place at the Banquet in the Penthouse of 'The Riviera Hotel and Casino.'

I managed to squeeze into my Black Velvet, Bird of Paradise suit. It was the one I had designed myself and had made in 'Granny takes a trip Boutique,' in Kings Road, Chelsea in 1970. About 35 years earlier. I also wore a long blond wig - it made me look more like me. As pretty as I hoped I looked, the Bride was breathtaking - my lovely Linda.

I was standing between Father Sanderson - who used to wrestle as 'The Wolf-man' before he became an ordained Catholic Priest, and my Best-Man, Don Leo Jonathan, a wrestler who had inspired me for a half a century.

The sound of 'The Wedding March' began - played on the piano by Joey Boesch, son of my friend Paul Boesch, who was a wrestling promoter from Houston, Texas. Joey at this time, had his own show at 'The Barbary Coast Hotel and Casino.

Then here comes the Beautiful Bride, escorted by the man who was to give her away, - Karl Lauer, one of the first two promoters that we wrestled for in The United States of America.

I cried - the Bride laughed. It was absolutely surreal, and a very long journey for the 15 year old Coalminer with outlandish dreams.

THE PALAIS DE TOKYO - PARIS, FRANCE. FROM ONE REVOLUTION TO ANOTHER.

Jeremy Deller is an English conceptual video installation Artist. Turner Prize Winner 2004 and in 2010 was awarded the Albert Medal of The Royal Society for Encouragements of Arts, Manufactures & Commerce. I regarded Jeremy as Britain's answer to Andy Warhol, who Jeremy met in 1986. I first heard of Jeremy when he contacted me to ask my permission to use, the now very famous photograph I had taken at a coalmine. It was the coalmine where my Father worked for 51 years and I had began work there, at my Father's insistence aged 15. Both he, and all the other coal miners ridiculed my dreams of becoming a professional Wrestler. It was for that reason that after winning the European Middleweight Wrestling Title, I insisted that the photos of me wearing my newly won Championship Belt would be taken with my Father, at that very coalmine. The coalmine that he had forced me to work at when I was just a little Boy with very BIG dreams. They say one picture is worth a thousand words - that photo has to be worth a million, as it hasn't stop yapping since it was taken back in 1974.

After his great success at the Palais De Tokyo, Jeremy called me again, this time to talk to me about his plans to film a documentary of my Life story. He came out to stay with us in November 2008 to talk about the project he had in mind. He told me that the film would be shown in a Film Festival that was going to take place in Rio De Janiero, Brazil. He returned early the next year with a cameraman, and our documentary began. The quote I often used when confronting an opponent 'I have so many ways to hurt you - you'll have to invent new ways to scream.' amused Jeremy and he decided to name the documentary film 'So many ways to hurt you.' Which, incidentally is also the title of the third book of my autobiography.

SO MANY WAYS TO HURT YOU

THE LIFE AND TIMES OF ADRIAN STREET By Jeremy Deller.

Adrian Street is a wrestler I first became aware of through a photograph showing him with his Father in 1974, which seemed to me, possibly the most important photograph taken post-war. It encapsulates the whole history of Britain for that period - of our uneasy transition from being the centre of heavy industry to a producer of entertainment and services. It's a rather bizarre and disturbing photograph, taken when Adrian went back to Wales, to the mine he had worked in as a young man, to meet his Father. Adrian's still very much alive and still wrestling in Florida, where he has settled. He's an incredible person, who has tremendous willpower and a great sense of his own worth' His story has an epic quality to it, he has basically reinvented himself for the late twentieth century.

My documentary film ran for about 7 months in Rio De Janiero, after which it travelled to London's Hayward Gallery. Everywhere it has shown, they had local artists paint huge murals depicting their concept of my life's journey. The cities where it traveled would also have 30 foot high photos of the coalmine plastered everywhere. After the Hayward Gallery it has shown in many major cities in Britain. It has also traveled to Belgium, Spain, Venice, Italy, Japan, Bosnia. In the States it ran in Philadelphia, New York and St. Louis. As I write this, it's showing in Mexico City, where the huge mural painted by a local Artist shows me depicted as an 'AZTEC GOD' tearing the living heart out of an opponent's chest. I have to say that being an Aztec God certainly beats the HELL out of being a scruffy little Welsh Coalminer.

****

In spite of my many career ending injuries and an almost life ending illness, I had survived them all. I decided that when the curtain finally came down on my wrestling career, I would do it strictly on my own terms - the way I had always done things. It would be my call and mine alone. In 2010 at the age of 70, I fought Ricky 'The Rocket' Roberts for the NWA Alabama Heavyweight Wrestling Championship - I won it of course. Then I continued to defend it against all comers.

If there was anything I really dreaded, it was the fact that I knew that one day my career would end. From my very first contest in 1957 at the age of 16, I knew that one day, as I stood in my corner of the ring, that this contest would be my last. I dreaded that day like one would dread death. But things and attitudes change. I was now over 72 years of age and had a contest coming up in Jasper, Alabama, on what would have been my Father's 103rd Birthday. The 9th of March 2013. I decided almost at the last minute, that it was at last the time to call it quits. I would be wrestling in a tag-team contest. Jimmy Golden and myself against 'The Exotic Ones,' Simon Sermon and Rick Michaels. As their team's name suggests, they had adopted my persona. They wore Exotic makeup, Exotic costumes, they acted flamboyantly effeminate. It seemed somehow symbolic to pass the torch to two wrestlers who would carry on utilizing a great persona, even if they did get the crap beaten out of them in the process. When the contest was over, I gave both my opponents one of my wrestling boots each, as a souvenir of my last professional Wrestling contest. - Or what I had intended to be my last professional wrestling contest.

When word went around that I had at last retired, the news caused a major uproar. I got an avalanche of offers to 'Wrestle one more time.'

"If I'd known it was going to be your last contest, I would have been there for sure!" I heard over and over.

I must admit that I hadn't really given the fans a lot of notice, with the result my last contest was missed by so very many loyal fans, who would have been there if they had been told in time. When Linda Marx asked me to do just one more, I decided I would and go out with much more FANFARE!!!

The date of my last contest was June 14th 2014, I was 73 years old. The venue was Graysville, Alabama. The last opponent of my 57 year wrestling career, would be Aeonn Flexx, who had been a pupil and trainer at Skullkrushers Wrestling School. Aeonn was an excellent opponent - But I won my final contest and retired as NWA Alabama Heavyweight Champion. After the contest Linda and I were then presented with a beautiful Italian Crystal Cup, by promoter and friend Linda Marx. It was inscribed - 'WRESTLE BIRMINGHAM presents to the EXOTIC ADRIAN STREET and MISS LINDA - THIS LIFETIME AWARD FOR YOUR DEDICATION TO THE SPORT OF WRESTLING. JUNE 14th 2014. THANKS FOR THE MEMORIES.

Thank you Linda Marx - first class all the way.

Our full time business nowadays, is costume designing and creation. We make costumes for all kinds of showbiz folk, although mostly for wrestlers. We also do a lot for Circus performers. We designed and created all the costumes for Mickey Rourke and the other actors, who played wrestlers in the movie 'The Wrestler.'

Just recently we deigned an outfit for ex Soldier, Troy Walsingham, who wrestles as 'The Wounded Warrior.' Troy was a Squad Designated Marksman. Infantry - M14 EBR [Enhanced Battle Rifle] Specialist E4. During action in the Kunar Province in Northern Afghanistan, Troy had his right arm blown off, just below his elbow. As Troy was awarded 'The Purple Heart' we designed a camouflage outfit with a large Purple heart emblem on his chest. When Troy handed me the Purple Heart medal, in order for me to more accurately copy it in metallic purple and gold fabric, I cried. In fact I sobbed my heart out. Troy is a real life Hero, I can't stress enough how much respect I have for him and others who have sacrificed so much for their country. Also, he is a Man who will not let anything stand in the way of his dream, of becoming a professional wrestler. Troy is the living proof, that anyone can do whatever they want to do - but you really have to want to do it.

Although I am now officially retired as a wrestler, both Linda and I are still in great demand to make special appearances at various wrestling shows etc. In March 2015 we were 'Special

Guests at 'Pensacon,' which was promoted by Mike Ensley, and held at Pensacola's Bayfront Centre.

Linda and I were 'Special guests,' and we were set up with a large table, from where we would meet and greet, sign autographs and have our photos taken with fans. On our right was our old Mate, Don Fargo, on our left was 'Hacksaw' Jim Duggan. Next to Jim Duggan was Rae-Dawn Chong. I hadn't seen Rae-Dawn since we were in Kenya, East Africa, where we starred together in 'Quest for Fire.' That was 35 years ago. Sgt. Slaughter was next to Don Fargo, but as we were quite cramped, he moved his table just outside our room. He was then right next to Naomi Grossman, one of the Stars of 'American Horror Story.' Other Stars in our room included 'Tiny' Lister, who also played 'Zeus' for the WWE. Tony Todd who was 'The Candyman.' Herbert Jefferson Jr. who was Lieutenant Boomer, in 'Battlestar Galactica.' In another room was Finn Jones, Daniel Portman and Gethin Anthony all starring in one of my favorite shows, 'Game of Thrones.' Also David Fielding who played 'Zordon' in 'Power Rangers.' The Giant Carel Struychen who played 'Lurch' and the Midget Felix Silla who played 'Cousin It' in 'The Adams Family.' We made friends with Robert D'Zar, who played the title role in 'Maniac Cop.' We both agreed that a good action movie, and a good action wrestling contest, is only as hot as it's hottest villain. And Robert was most definitely a hot villain. On our last day Robert became ill, so ill in fact that he collapsed and had to be taken to a Hospital in Pensacola. He died there a couple of days later.

Whilst on this very sad subject, my first regular tag-team partner back in the 60s, Tony Charles died on March 13th 2015. Tony and his Wife Pam, lived about 20 miles from us. We often got together over all the years we have both lived in Gulf Breeze. We will really miss him.

On September 15th 2014, I became a Granddad for the 4th time, When my oldest Son Adrian Jr. and his wife Charlotte had their first Baby. A lovely little Baby Girl, named Tallulah-Mae. If this gorgeous little creature takes after her Mum and Dad, she will have a beautiful singing voice when she grows up - you mark my words!

Linda and I celebrated our 10th Wedding Anniversary, by returning to the scene of the crime, 'The Cauliflower Alley Club Reunion' in Las Vegas. My oldest wrestling friend Tony Scarlo and his Wife Rose, flew out from the UK, to help us Celebrate. Bishop Jason Sanderson, who married us was also there. So was Joey Boesch who played the wedding march at our Wedding, with his Mother Shirley. Also Karl Lauer, who was one of the first two promoters I wrestled for in the States, who had 'given the Bride away.' All we needed to complete the original cast, would have been Don Leo Jonathan, who was my Best Man, and my earliest inspiration in professional wrestling.

This is the 7th book of my autobiography - as I write this, there is a proposed musical stage play - 'Exotic Adrian - The Musical.' and a feature film 'Adrian' in the works, both inspired by my books and my life.

I had been born into a dark, grey, violent World. World War II was raging. Everyone was hungry, everyone was unhappy - everything was colorless. My Father was a prisoner of War with the Japanese in Java, then Sumatra. When the war ended, I was almost 5 years of age. My Father, who I had longed for, returned. I thought that I would be happy then. But - for whatever reason, my Father didn't like me. He made my childhood very lonely and very sad. He had me out of school and working in the coal mine when I was 15 years old. During the war everything had been grey. Now everything was black. The pit was dark, unhealthy and dangerous. If you worked in the mines you would remain anonymous, for whatever remained of your dreary, miserable life. When I declared that I was determined to change my whole way of life, everyone I knew scoffed and ridiculed my dreams. They would all one day learn that THEY had steeled my determination - they unintentionally guaranteed my eventual success. I was determined to prove them all wrong. I had survived the seven deadly Cs - Childbirth - Childhood - Chapel - Coalmine - Criticism - Crabtrees and Cancer. Now I would make the World for myself, and everyone who would ever hear of me, a much more colorful place to live. In spite of - or because of, my very many detractors. I am confident I achieved my goal in life.

Life is like a Carousel - sometimes you're up and sometimes you're down. And sometimes you just go round and round. Just remember - enjoy the ride.

PHOTOS

1984 BLEED'N HELL!!!

1984 Crockett's Promotion.

1984 Jim Crockett's Promotion.

1984 SADISTS IN SEQUINS.

'GRUNT'
The Wrestling Movie
1985

1985 'Grunt' the Wrestling Movie.

1985 - Giant Lady Maxine.

1985 Demolishing the Giant Lady Maxine.

HOLYWOOD HILLS
1985

1985 Liberace and I.

1985 Our closet.

1985 Picking up a few tips.

1985 Posing with my own copy of a Frank Frazzetta.

1985 Southeastern Heavyweight Champion.

1985 Tag-partner the Giant Marine - Stan Fraiser. He later became Uncle Elmer.

1985 Tagging with Moondog.

1985 The Cramps' 'Clown Painting' by Serial Killer, John Wayne Gacey.

1985 Vince - Jimmy Maslon - Adrian Jr. - Cramps -Poison Ivy & Lux.

1985 Vince - Linda - Mandy - Adrian Jr. in Las Vegas.

Hoover Dam 1985

1985 With my Kids at Hoover Dam.

1986 British look.

1986 'Royal Pink Wrestling Belt.'

1986 I'm Relaxing with my oils.

1986 Isn't that Grand!

Kevin Sullivan and the Fallen Angel

1986 Kevin Sullivan wearing the Leather Headgear I made for him with 'Fallen Angel' Nancy.

1986 Kris Von Colt.

1986 Linda Lovely in Leather & Lace.

1986 My 'Royal' Pink Wrestling Belt.

1986 My 1st record Album 'Shake Wrestle 'n' Roll.'

1986 The 'Royal' Pink Wrestling Belt.

1986 Tiger - Tiger burning bright!

1986 Up yours!

1986-87 'Hustler' Rip Rogers - Best feud ever.

1987 Hawaii Diamondhead in the background.

1987 - Hawaii.

1987 - Hawaii.

1987 - Hawaii.

1987 Dazzler.

1987 Well hello Halo.

1988 - Dressed to KILL!

1988 - Legs like a Dancer - Linda's are nice too!

1988 Beautiful but Deadly.

BRUISER BRODY

1988 Bruiser Brody & I would have wrestled against Sheik Ed Farhat & The Iron Sheik if he hadn't been murdered in Puerto Rico.

1988 Sheik Ed Farhat stabs Dory Funk Jr.

The
SHEIK
U.S. HEAVYWEIGHT
CHAMPION

THE SHEIK

1988 Sheik Ed Farhat.

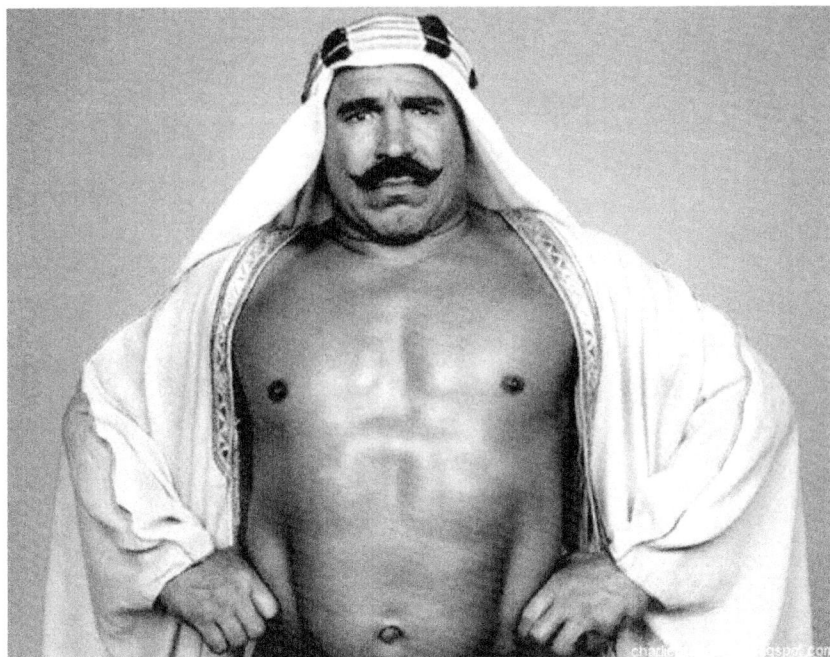

1988 The Iron Sheik.

1988 THE LITTLE 'EXOTIC FAN.'

1989 'Shake Wrestle 'n' Roll Concert.

1989 'Shake Wrestle 'n' Roll.'

1989 Luna - probably Linda's creepiest opponent.

1989 Striped for ACTION!

1989 When I wrestled Tony Atlas, Tony won the posing contest -
I won the Wrestling contest.

1990 Linda in Leather.

1990 Merchants of Menace.

1990 Wait until they get a load of me!!!

1991 Yet another 'Gender-Bender!'

1992 Amazon Queen.

1992 Dastardly Duo.

1992 Linda at Skullkrushers.

1992 Linda the Warrior.

1992 World's Best Valet.

1993 LPWA - Roles reversed.

1993 LPWA Beating Iraqi Sheik Adnan Al-Kaissie.

1994 Me with Al Costello & The New Kangaroos.

1994 Tag-Partner Don Jardine - The Spoiler.

1994 The Spoiler demonstrates his Claw - OUCH!!!

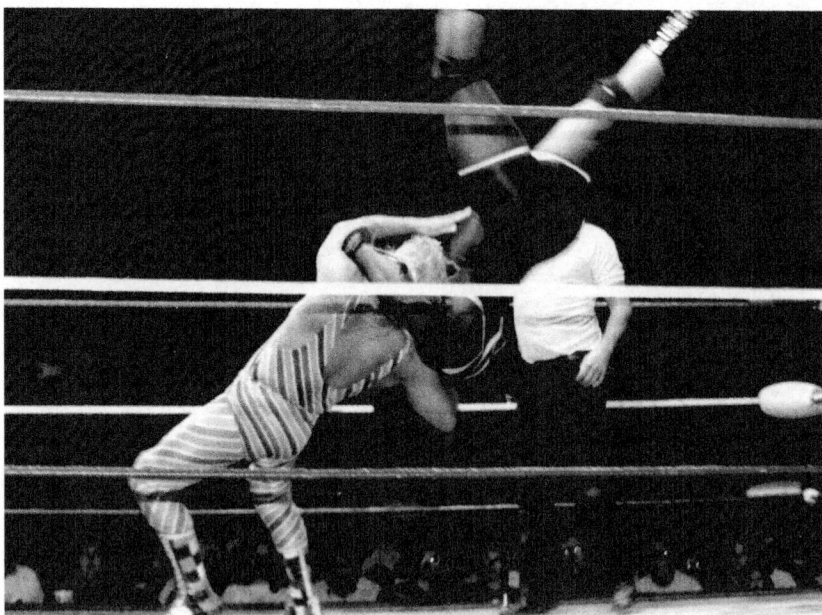

1997 Soften them up with a suplex!

1997 Then pin them with a London Bridge.

1999 Mick Foley at Skullkrushers.

2000 My 60th Birthday.

2000 Posing with two trophies of my victories.

2000 Working out at Mick Foley's Gym.

2001 Me vs. Thunderkat - my hair against Thunderkat's Mask.

2001 Me with Thunderkat's Mask.

2002 Joyce Grable - Linda - Fabulous Moolah - Me - in front
Diamond Lil.

2002 with Steven Regal and Triple H.

2003 With the Undertaker - The Big Show & Vince McMahon.

2004 Our own Garden of Eden.

2004 We have Birds, Bees, Buterflies & Bears.

2005 - World Champions.

2005 - World Mixed Tagteam Champions.

2005 Bruno Sammartino - Me - 'Cowboy' Bill Watts.

2005 My Best Man Don Leo Jonathan.

2005 My first meeting with Best Man Don Leo Jonathan.

2005 Our Wedding - Father Jason Sanderson Aka 'Wolfman.'

2005 Our Wedding Las Vegas.

2005 RINGSPORT AWARD.

2006 Cauliflower Alley with my old opponent Mil Mascarras.

2006 Cauliflower Alley with 'The Masked Destroyer.'

2007 Fighting in Florence.

2007 My Son Adrian plays Buddy Holly in the musical 'BUDDY.'

2008 Navarre Beach.

2008 vs RICKY ROCKET.

2009 Gulf Coast Reunion with Don Fargo & Ole Anderson.

2009 Gulf Coast Reunion with Ole' Anderson.

NWA ALABAMA
HEAVYWEIGHT
CHAMPION 2010

2010 NWA Alabama Heavyweight Champion.

2010 Winning the NWA Alabama Heavyweight Title.

2011 Tony Charles' 76th Birthday.

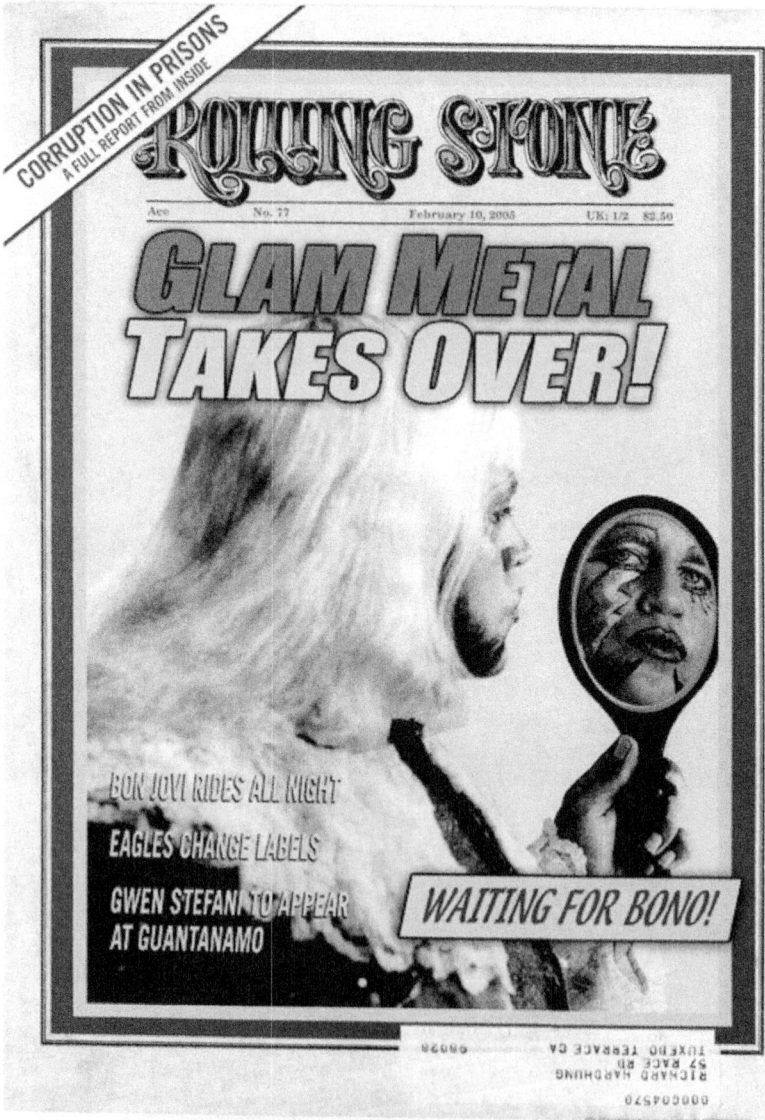

2012 A painting by Bob Dylan.

2012 Defending my NWA Alabama Heavyweight Title.

2013 'So many ways to hurt you.' PHILADELPHIA-NEW
YORK-ST LOUIS -Deller.

2013 Defeating Simon Sermon in what was almost my last contest.

2014 'So many ways to hurt you' Manchester.

2014 'So many ways to hurt you.' Jeremy Deller at Manchester's Life and Times of Exotic Adrian Street.

2014 Jack Brisco gets amorous.

2014 Jim Cornett & Ox Baker.

2014 Lifetime Wrestling Awards after my last Pro Contest June 14th.

2014 Poster of My last Professional Contest.

2015 'The Wounded Warrior' real life hero poses with his Purple Heart outfit.

2015 'Wildcat' Wendall Cooley - Me - 'Bullet' Bob Armstrong - Linda. Robert Gibson behind.

2015 Me as an Aztec God 'So many Ways to hurt you' in Mexico.

2015 Pensacon 'Game of Thrones' Daniel Portman.

2015 Pensacon 'Game of Thrones' Gethin Anthony.

Finn Jones
Game of Thrones

2015 Pensacon 'Game of Thrones' Finn Jones.

Robert
Z' Dar

2015 Pensacon 'Maniac Cop' Robert D'Zar.

2015 Pensacon 'Quest for Fire' Rae-Dawn Chong.

2015 Pensacon Adams Family.

2015 Pensacon Hacksaw Jim Duggan.

2015 Pensacon Herbert Jefferson Jr. - 'Battlestar Galactica.'

2015 Pensacon Niomi Grossman 'American Horror.'

2015 Pensacon Sgt Slaughter.

2015 Pensacon Tony Todd 'CANDYMAN.'

2015 Pensacon Zordon 'Power Rangers.'

Oil 0001.

Oil 0002.

Oil 0005.

Pastel 0005.

Pastel 1001a.

Pastel 2000a.

Pastel 2001a.

Pastel 3002a.

Pastel 4000.

Pastel 4003.

ADRIAN STREET

Printed in Great Britain
by Amazon

86428678R00169